Th[e ~]
MOTHERS

A PRAYER BOOK
FOR ORTHODOX MOMS

Annalisa Boyd

Ancient Faith Publishing

Chesterton, Indiana

Unless otherwise noted, Scripture quotations are taken from
the New King James Version, © 1979, 1980, 1982 by Thomas
Nelson, Inc. Used by permission.

Published by:
    Ancient Faith Publishing
    (*formerly known as Conciliar Press*)
    A Division of Ancient Faith Ministries
    P.O. Box 748
    Chesterton, IN 46304

Printed in the United States of America

ISBN 10: 1-936270-95-1
ISBN 13: 978-1-936270-95-8

This book is dedicated to one of the

most amazing mothers I have ever known:

Khouria Terry Elizabeth Beck 1952—2012

Wife—Mother—Friend

May her memory be eternal!

Special thanks to:

Fr. David Mustain, Maryfaith Woods,

Christina Louwers,

and my own mama, Bonnie Johnstone

Contents

INDEX TO PROFILES OF SAINTS

A Prayer for Mothers

O Lord Jesus Christ our God, who came into this world not to be served but to serve and to give Your life as a ransom for many: Help me, I beseech You, in my ministry of caring for the children You have given me. Enable me to be patient in tribulations, to instruct with a meek and gentle spirit, to reprimand with inner tranquility and a sober mind, and to serve in humility of heart with love. May I thus live in You alone, by You alone, and for You alone, showing forth Your virtues and leading my family on the path of Your saving commandments, that we may glorify You, together with Your unoriginate Father and Your all-holy and life-giving Spirit, both in this world and that which is to come. Amen.[1]

Prayer is a great weapon, a rich treasure, a wealth that is never exhausted, an undisturbed refuge, a cause of tranquility, the root of a multitude of blessings and their source.
—*St. John Chrysostom*

Introduction

A T THE TIME OF THE PRINTING OF THIS BOOK, I will have given birth to three, adopted five, fostered thirty, and been godmother to five children. And still I'm no expert! Whether you are mother to one child or fifteen, it is important to note that once you welcome a child into your life, you will never be the same. From the time that child enters your life—however that child enters your life—your whole worldview shifts.

These precious gifts can be the cause of great joy, great frustration, and great pain. But if we embrace it all "for the joy set before us" (see Heb. 12:2), we will find even greater comfort from the One who created our children. In our Liturgy the priest says, "O Lord our God, Your power is incomparable. Your glory is incomprehensible. Your mercy is immeasurable. Your love for mankind is inexpressible." God's love for our children is wider and deeper and stronger than even the wide, deep, strong love of a mother.

The prayers in chapter two of this book are those prescribed by the Church. They have been written by the Fathers of the Church and have been found to be acceptable and beneficial in the official life of the Church. These, then, are the most important to pray and take to heart. Many of the other prayers throughout the book are simply prayers from the heart of one mama to another. While the other prayers in this book have been evaluated and approved by a priest, they are not the official prayers of the Church and should, therefore, be used for encouragement and to promote your own personal prayer time with our Lord.

I pray you will find comfort here to help you on your quest as you bring up your children in the way they should go, so that when they are grown they will not depart from it (Prov. 22:6).

MAKING TIME FOR PRAYER

You may have heard of Susanna Wesley, a godly mama who lived in the late seventeenth and early eighteenth centuries. Susanna had nineteen children. Even in a time before television, internet, and soccer practice, this mama was busy! How on earth did she find time to pray?

The children were given a signal so they knew when mama was praying. When she sat down and put her apron up over her head, they knew not to interrupt her until that apron came down. The important thing wasn't the amount of time she spent praying, but the fact that she set aside even a brief moment to be present before the Lord.

While we won't necessarily throw an apron over our heads, giving our children proof that we have finally lost it, we can find moments in the midst of our busy lives to pray and be still.

When contemplating the "how" of prayer life, it can be hard to wade through the obstacles we face on a daily basis. On the one hand, we believe our loving God can make a way for us to meet with Him each day. On the other hand, we face so many interruptions along with real responsibilities. If we don't tend to them, who will? Should we give up trying if we happen to be a morning person or have developed adult-onset ADD (I'm only partially kidding)? Is it only possible to be successful if we follow a particular formula? As mothers, sometimes we have to get creative.

I used to be a night person, and for many years I'd fall asleep while in the process of trying to do my devotions at night. I'd get a few prayers in and find myself mixing prayers and nonsense words, to the amusement of my husband. Years into marriage and motherhood, I became a group leader for a women's Bible study. I had a lovely group of women I was committed to pray for, but I kept forgetting, or I'd start falling asleep before all their names were mentioned.

I had to do something drastic. This night-mama started

getting up an hour before my children. Do you know what happened? Over the years I have become a morning person! I didn't believe it possible. The blessing and closeness with Christ this brought me were incredible. Each time I was successful in getting myself up early, I would find other moments throughout the day to pray or read a scripture verse to think on as I went about tending to the daily cares of my home.

Have I always been faithful in prayer? No. I have gone through spells where prayer felt almost like torture. It was dry and forced. But forced does not equate to unfruitful. Many times it is in the desert where we are most strengthened, and much good fruit is produced on the other end of those dry times—in spite of, or perhaps because of, the struggle.

Each mother is her own person with her own struggles and strengths. Your prayer time may look very different from mine. You may get up early in the morning to pray. You may stay up later (without falling asleep like me). You may be able to pray the hours each day. Or it may be all you can do to say one "Lord, have mercy on me, a sinner" with focus and sincerity. The point is to pray, to submit ourselves to Christ and trust He will make a way, if we are willing. Each of us needs to seek the counsel of our own spiritual mother or father, for God has placed these people in our lives to help us learn to run the race Christ has set before us with perseverance.

May the God of all creation, who blessed us with the children we have and knows the challenges we face each day, bless our time and provide a way for us to meet with Him each day. May He, as Metropolitan Philaret wrote, "pray Himself within me."

The Asceticism of Mothers

THE "RULE" OF MOTHERHOOD

OKAY, DON'T GET SCARED. THIS ISN'T WHERE I launch into all the things you've done wrong in your parenting or tell you that if you "just follow these simple steps you too can have the perfect children." You won't be criticized for the things you "should have done" when your children were little, being tortured with the idea that all hope is gone for your older children because you somehow missed the window. As Christians we are challenged to live in the now. For us as mothers, this is imperative if we are to be effective in our Christian walk and in our parenting.

I heard it said once that motherhood is a type of asceticism. Like the ascetics, mothers find themselves in a situation that requires their utter devotion, self-denial, daily emotional exercises, facing extreme challenges, and much prayer. I have read about the lives of many saints who became brides of Christ and lived as monastics. The idea of being able to spend sustained time in prayer or the reading of the Holy Scriptures made me wonder how on earth a lay person—a mother—could possibly contend with this world and reach that heavenly finish line Saint Paul talks about.

After expressing this concern to the mother abbess of a monastery, I was relieved when she responded with this quotation.

> *You greatly delude yourself and err, if you think that one thing is demanded from the layman and another from the monk; since the difference between them is in that whether one is married or not, while in everything else they have the same responsibilities. . . . Because all must rise to the same height; and what has turned the world upside down is that we think only the monk must live rigorously, while the rest are allowed to live a life of indolence. (St. John Chrysostom)*

When we accept a little child (or bigger one) in His name, we are accepting the ascetic life of motherhood. The "rules" of motherhood include the two commandments Christ gave: "The first of all the commandments *is*: '. . . And you shall love the LORD your God with all your heart, with all your soul, with all your mind, and with all your strength.' This *is* the first commandment. And the second, like *it, is* this: 'You shall love your neighbor as yourself.' There is no other commandment greater than these" (Mark 12:29–31).

How do we apply these commandments to the mothering of our children? Consider the virtues taught by the Church and how they apply to your own life. These are spiritual habits we can pursue at any time. They are tools to help us as we endeavor to work out our salvation with fear and trembling (Phil. 2:12), both for the salvation of our own souls and so that we may be light-bearers for our children as we help them walk along the way. Each "rule" is given with the understanding that you will seek out the guidance of your own spiritual advisor, the person who knows you and your life and family situation, for specific ways to walk forward in Christ.

THE VIRTUES

Humility ✌

Humility is the weapon used against pride. It is thinking of others before yourself. You might be thinking, "Wait, I'm a mom. I'm *always* thinking of others before myself!" I agree. We do spend a lot of time thinking of our children and providing for them day in and day out. Humility is tied in with the virtue of happiness. When Christ endured the cross, it was "for the joy set before Him" (from Heb. 12:2).

Letting our joy be evident as we serve in our homes or in our churches shows our children the blessing that comes from service. We may be the first to volunteer to bring a sick parishioner a meal or to clean up after fellowship time or to head the bake sale, but if we resent the service, we are not serving in humility. Likewise, if we refuse to volunteer for the little tasks because we have expertise in "more important" areas, we miss the mark as well. Remember the publican and the Pharisee. Both went to the temple to pray, but only one humbled himself. Let us always keep in our minds the Jesus prayer, "Lord Jesus Christ, Son of God, have mercy on *me,* a sinner."

Liberality ᔡ

Liberality is living generously; it serves as a weapon against greed. Give freely to others when it is within your power to do so, without any expectation of getting something in return. This includes giving to the homeless, friends, enemies, neighbors, and those in our own families. We can't simply expect this from our children. We model it when they watch us joyfully give to others and when they are the recipients of our generosity. And we can help them live generously by providing opportunities for them to give or serve.

Chastity ॐ

Chastity is a weapon against lust; it isn't only for virgins. Chastity is purity of heart, mind, and body. This means being mindful of what we watch, read, listen to, and say. We don't want to hide our heads in the sand or make some alternate reality for our children, but we do want them to understand the world around them in a loving and godly context. How can we expect our children to control their passions if we aren't guarding our own eyes, mouths, and ears?

Mildness ॐ

Mildness is used to fight wrath and anger. It consists of kindness, gentleness, and calm in word and action. Whether you have one child or many children, home can become a chaotic place. Sometimes the chaos is the fact that all nine children have left their stuff all over the counters, chairs, and floors (nine people can produce a lot of stuff!). Many times the chaos comes from the emotional ups and downs our children face as they are learning to understand God, others, and themselves. Being the calm in one's home can mean the difference between ending the day with a yelling match or being able to honestly say, "Good night, honey, I love you." Mildness is closely related to temperance and humility because it requires a lot of self-control and humility to address the myriad of issues each home faces with kindness, gentleness, and calm. Of course there will be those days you are tempted to lock yourself in the closet and curl up in the fetal position, but the God of the universe is there on those days, too. As we seek the Lord through prayer and the observance of the sacraments, we can *be* the calm in our homes. His power is that big!

Temperance ൴

Temperance is a weapon against gluttony. Practicing self-control, moderation, and restraint as a mother sets a good example to your children in how they should approach life. These lessons are taught each church year through the observation and celebration of the fasts and feasts. Learning to celebrate without gorging ourselves helps us to appreciate the sacrifice of the fast and embrace the blessing of the feast.

Happiness ൴

Happiness protects us from envy. There is a time for great rejoicing and a time for sorrow. For Christians, even the times of sorrow are tempered with joy, because we know this world is temporary and we press on toward the world to come. We can help our children embrace happiness by being, well, happy. We can be happy because we are thankful to the Lord for all His blessings, for our family and for how He provides for us. We can also be happy for how He provides for others. The Bible tells us to rejoice in the Lord always. Because of His great sacrifice for us, we can truly rejoice even in the midst of trials.

Diligence ॐ

We use diligence to fight against sloth or laziness. Diligence is doing any task (work chore job responsibility) until it is completed to the very best of our ability. I once saw a funny story about a woman who went out one morning to water the plants, but while she was watering the plants she noticed her car needed to be washed. She put down the hose to go get the bucket, sponge, and soap, but when she reached for the soap she saw the car keys she had misplaced. She didn't want to lose them again, so she went to put her keys away in her purse, but when she headed to her bedroom to retrieve her purse, she passed the bathroom and saw her husband had left his dirty towel on the floor. She decided to put it in the hamper, which reminded her she needed to start a load of laundry. And so it went all day long. By the end of the day she was exhausted, but nothing seemed to have really gotten done, and she couldn't remember why the hose was running.

Now add children to the mix! Taking the time to complete a task is a worthy goal. Of course, as mothers, we have times when emergencies come up and plans must change, but if we strive to set the example of managing our time well so we *can* be diligent in our responsibilities, we will find it time well spent.

— 2 —

Daily Prayer

O NE OF MY FAVORITE STORIES ABOUT PRAYER comes from a little book called *The Prayer Rope*.[2] I love it because of the pious and wealthy man who became a monk but could not, for the life of him, remember even one of the prescribed prayers. Finally a fellow monk read him many short prayers and asked which he liked best. Through hard work, the other monks taught him the prayer he chose: "Rejoice, Mary, thou art full of grace; O Theotokos and Virgin, the Lord is with thee. Blessed art thou among women, and blessed is the Fruit of thy womb; for thou hast borne the Savior of our souls." After some time, he finally learned the prayer, and he was so pleased that all he said all the time was "Rejoice, Mary." Even the other monks began to call him Rejoice Mary.

Sometimes I feel so feeble in my efforts and beat myself

up for not remembering every prayer. Even after years of practice, some I only remember in the right context. Some I recognize but can't repeat. But I remember Rejoice Mary and think if I can remember even a little prayer and pray it honestly, perhaps the Lord will accept my small offering.

No matter how little time we feel we have, we can always take a moment to pray. Learning all or some of the daily prayers listed below will help you take advantage of even those fleeting moments to pray. And let us remember, "Prayer is a great weapon, a rich treasure, a wealth that is never exhausted, an undisturbed refuge, a cause of tranquility, the root of a multitude of blessings and their source" (St. John Chrysostom).

MORNING PRAYERS

The Trisagion Prayers ↝

In the Name of the Father, and of the Son, and of the Holy Spirit. Amen.

Glory to You, our God, glory to You.

O Heavenly King, O Comforter, the Spirit of truth, who are in all places and fill all things; Treasury of good things and Giver of Life: Come and dwell in us and cleanse us from every stain, and save our souls, O gracious Lord.

Holy God, Holy Mighty, Holy Immortal, have mercy on us.

Holy God, Holy Mighty, Holy Immortal, have mercy on us. Holy God, Holy Mighty, Holy Immortal, have mercy on us.

All-holy Trinity, have mercy on us. Lord, cleanse us from our sins. Master, pardon our iniquities. Holy God, visit and heal our infirmities for Your Name's sake.

Lord, have mercy. Lord, have mercy. Lord, have mercy.

Glory to the Father, and to the Son, and to the Holy Spirit, both now and ever and unto ages of ages. Amen.

Our Father, who are in heaven, hallowed be Your Name; Your Kingdom come; Your will be done on earth as it is in heaven. Give us this day our daily bread; and forgive us our trespasses, as we forgive those who trespass against us; and lead us not into temptation, but deliver us from evil.

For Yours is the Kingdom, and the power, and the glory of the Father, and the Son, and of the Holy Spirit; now and ever and unto ages of ages. Amen.

The Creed ॐ

I believe in one God, the Father Almighty, Maker of heaven and earth, and of all things visible and invisible.

And in one Lord Jesus Christ, the Son of God, the Only-begotten, Begotten of the Father before all worlds, Light of Light, Very God of Very God, begotten, not made; of one essence with the Father, by whom all things were made:

Who for us men and for our salvation came down from heaven, and was incarnate of the Holy Spirit and the Virgin Mary, and became man;

And was crucified also for us under Pontius Pilate, and suffered and was buried.

And the third day He rose again, according to the Scriptures;

And ascended into heaven, and sits at the right hand of the Father;

And He shall come again with glory to judge the living and the dead, whose kingdom shall have no end.

And I believe in the Holy Spirit, the Lord and Giver of Life, who proceeds from the Father, who with the Father and the Son together is worshipped and glorified, who spoke by the Prophets;

And I believe in One Holy Catholic and Apostolic Church. I acknowledge one Baptism for the remission of sins. I look for the resurrection of the dead and the Life of the world to come. Amen.

Prayer of Metropolitan Philaret ॐ

O Lord, grant that I may meet the coming day in peace. Help me in all things to rely upon Your holy will. In each hour of the day reveal Your will to me. Bless my dealings with all who surround me. Teach me to treat all that comes to me throughout the day with peace of soul, and with the firm conviction that Your will governs all. In all my deeds and words, guide my thoughts and feelings. In unforeseen events, let me not forget that all are sent by You. Teach me to act firmly and wisely, without embittering and embarrassing others. Give me the strength to bear the fatigue of the coming day with all that it shall bring. Direct my will. Teach me to pray. Pray within me.

Most Holy God, I pray and beseech You, give me a pure heart, a way of speaking that befits the faith I profess. Grant me uprightness of purpose, powers of reasoning unhindered by passions, conduct that becomes those who fear You, and perfect knowledge of Your commandments. May I enjoy health in body and in spirit. Grant me a life of peace, genuine faith and living hope, sincere charity and bountiful generosity, patience that knows no bounds, and the light of Your truth to proclaim Your goodness to me, that forever and in all things placing my trust only in You, I may abound in every good work, and that in Christ Your gifts may increase in every soul. For to You belong all glory, honor, and majesty, Father, Son, and Holy Spirit, now and ever and unto ages of ages. Amen.

Lord Jesus Christ, Son of God, have mercy on me, a sinner.
Lord Jesus Christ, Son of God, have mercy on me, a sinner.
Lord Jesus Christ, Son of God, have mercy on me, a sinner.

O my God and my King, have mercy on me and pardon my transgressions, both voluntary and involuntary, of word and of deed, and make me worthy to be Your simple servant, O gracious Lord.

O Father in heaven, forgive (*Name*). Instead of anything good I think I can do on my own, fill me with Your Holy Spirit and grant me Your love, joy, peace, longsuffering, kindness, goodness, gentleness, thankfulness, self-control, mercy, humility, wisdom, and the courage to walk in Your ways.

O holy Theotokos, save us. More honorable than the cherubim and more glorious beyond compare than the seraphim, you who without corruption bore God the Word and are truly Theotokos, we magnify you.

O holy lady, be my mother and place a hedge of protection around my heart, my mind, and my mouth that I may not sin against your Son.

As I rise up out of the dark, O lover of mankind, I beseech You, enlighten and guide me also in Your commandments, and teach me to always do Your will.

The Breastplate Prayer of St. Patrick ᷟ

I bind unto myself today
The Power of God to hold and lead,
His eye to watch, His might to stay,
His ear to hearken to my need.
The wisdom of my God to teach,
His hand to guide, His shield to ward;
The word of God to give me speech,
His heavenly host to be my guard.

Christ, be with me, Christ before me, Christ behind me.
Christ in me, Christ beneath me, Christ above me,
Christ on my right, Christ on my left,
Christ when I lie, Christ when I sit,
Christ when I arise,
Christ in the heart of every one who thinks of me,
Christ in the mouth of every one who speaks of me,
Christ in every eye that sees me,
Christ in every ear that hears me.

Salvation is of the Lord,
Salvation is of the Christ.
May Your salvation, O Lord, be ever with us.

A Prayer to the Holy Trinity ༄

Arising from sleep, I thank You, O Holy Trinity, that because of the riches of Your goodness and longsuffering, in Your compassion You raised me up as I lay in hopelessness; that in the morning I might sing the glories of Your Majesty.

Now guide the eyes of my understanding, open my mouth to receive Your words, teach me Your commandments, help me to do Your will, confessing You from my heart, singing and praising Your All-holy Name: of the Father, and of the Son, and of the Holy Spirit: now and ever and unto ages of ages. Amen.

MIDDAY PRAYERS

The Trisagion Prayers ༄

In the Name of the Father, and of the Son, and of the Holy Spirit. Amen.

Glory to You, our God, glory to You.

O Heavenly King, O Comforter, the Spirit of truth, who are in all places and fill all things; Treasury of good things and Giver of Life: Come and dwell in us and cleanse us from every stain, and save our souls, O gracious Lord.

Holy God, Holy Mighty, Holy Immortal, have mercy on us.
Holy God, Holy Mighty, Holy Immortal, have mercy on us.
Holy God, Holy Mighty, Holy Immortal, have mercy on us.

All-holy Trinity, have mercy on us. Lord, cleanse us from our sins. Master, pardon our iniquities. Holy God, visit and heal our infirmities for Your Name's sake.

Lord, have mercy. Lord, have mercy. Lord, have mercy.

Glory to the Father, and to the Son, and to the Holy Spirit, both now and ever and unto ages of ages. Amen.

Our Father, who are in heaven, hallowed be Your Name; Your Kingdom come; Your will be done on earth as it is in heaven. Give us this day our daily bread; and forgive us our trespasses, as we forgive those who trespass against us; and lead us not into temptation, but deliver us from evil.

For Yours is the Kingdom, and the power, and the glory of the Father, and the Son, and of the Holy Spirit; now and ever and unto ages of ages. Amen.

O Christ my God, who at this hour stretched out Your loving arms upon the cross so that all men might be gathered unto Yourself, help me and save me, who cry out to You: Glory to You, O Lord.

Through the prayers of our holy Fathers, Lord Jesus Christ our God, have mercy upon me and save me. Amen.

EVENING PRAYERS

The Trisagion Prayers ᔆ

In the Name of the Father, and of the Son, and of the Holy Spirit. Amen.

Glory to You, our God, glory to You.

O Heavenly King, O Comforter, the Spirit of truth, who are in all places and fill all things; Treasury of good things and Giver of Life: Come and dwell in us and cleanse us from every stain, and save our souls, O gracious Lord.

Holy God, Holy Mighty, Holy Immortal, have mercy on us.
Holy God, Holy Mighty, Holy Immortal, have mercy on us.
Holy God, Holy Mighty, Holy Immortal, have mercy on us.

All-holy Trinity, have mercy on us. Lord, cleanse us from our sins. Master, pardon our iniquities. Holy God, visit and heal our infirmities for Your Name's sake.

Lord, have mercy. Lord, have mercy. Lord, have mercy.

Glory to the Father, and to the Son, and to the Holy Spirit, both now and ever and unto ages of ages. Amen.

Our Father, who are in heaven, hallowed be Your Name; Your Kingdom come; Your will be done on earth as it is in heaven. Give us this day our daily bread; and forgive us our trespasses, as we forgive those who trespass against us; and lead us not into temptation, but deliver us from evil.

For Yours is the Kingdom, and the power, and the glory of the Father, and the Son, and of the Holy Spirit, now and ever and unto ages of ages. Amen.

Troparia of Thanksgiving ॐ

Now that the day has come to a close, I thank You, O Lord, and I ask that the evening with the night may be sinless; grant this to me, O Savior, and save me.

Glory to the Father, and to the Son, and to the Holy Spirit.

Now that the day has passed, I glorify You, O Master, and I ask that the evening with the night may be without wrongdoing; grant this to me, O Savior, and save me.

Both now and ever, and unto ages of ages. Amen.

Now that the day has run its course, I praise You, O Holy One, and I ask that the evening with the night may be undisturbed; grant this to me, O Savior, and save me.

Lord have mercy. *(12x)*

A Prayer for Forgiveness ❧

O Lord our God, if during this day I have sinned, whether in word or deed or thought, forgive me all, for You are good and love mankind. Grant me peaceful and undisturbed sleep, and deliver me from the temptations of the evil one. Raise me up again in the morning that I may glorify You; for You are blessed, with Your Only-begotten Son and Your All-Holy Spirit: now and ever, and unto ages of ages. Amen.

In All Seasons and in Every Hour ❧

O Christ our God, who at all times and in every hour, in heaven and on earth, are worshiped and glorified; who are long-suffering, merciful, and compassionate; who love the righteous and show mercy to the sinner; who call all to salvation through the promise of blessings to come: O Lord, in this hour receive our humble prayers, and direct our lives according to Your commandments. Make holy our souls, bless our bodies, correct our thoughts, cleanse our minds; deliver us from all suffering, evil, and distress. Surround us with Your holy angels, that guided and guarded by them, we may attain to the unity of the faith and to the knowledge of Your unapproachable glory, for You are blessed unto ages of ages. Amen.

St. Augustine's Evening Prayer ᴈ

Watch, dear Lord, with those who wake, or watch, or weep tonight, and give Your angels charge over those who sleep. Tend Your sick ones, O Lord Christ, rest Your weary ones. Bless Your dying ones. Soothe Your suffering ones. Pity Your afflicted ones. Shield Your joyous ones. And all for Your love's sake. Amen.

The Jesus Prayer ᴈ

Lord Jesus Christ, Son of God, have mercy on me, a sinner.

Prayer to Your Guardian Angel ᴈ

O angel of God, my holy guardian, given to me from heaven, enlighten me this day and save me from all evil. Instruct me in doing good deeds and set me on the path of salvation. Amen.

O angel of Christ, holy guardian and protector of my soul and body, forgive me everything wherein I have offended you every day of my life, and protect me from all influence and temptation of the evil one. May I never again anger God by my sins. Pray for me to the Lord, that He may make me worthy of the grace of the All-Holy Trinity, and of the blessed Mother of God, and of all the saints. Amen.

Prayer to Your Patron Saint ᴈ

Pray to God for me, O Holy Saint *(Name)*, for you are well-pleasing to God: for I turn to you, who are the speedy helper and intercessor for my soul.

Prayer to the All-Holy Trinity ❧

The Father is my hope; the Son is my refuge; the Holy Spirit is my protector. O All-holy Trinity, glory to You.

Hymn to the Theotokos ❧

It is truly right to bless you, O Theotokos, who are ever blessed and all-blameless and the mother of our God. More honorable than the cherubim, and more glorious beyond compare than the seraphim, you who without corruption bore God the Word and are truly Theotokos: we magnify you.

Lenten Prayer of St. Ephraim ❧

O Lord and Master of my life! Take from me the spirit of sloth, faint-heartedness, lust of power, and idle talk.

But give rather the spirit of chastity, humility, patience, and love to Your servant.

Yea, Lord and King! Grant me to see my own errors and not to judge my brother, for You are blessed unto ages of ages. Amen.

Tea Time at the Abyss

Prayers in Time of Trouble

*Stand at the brink of the abyss of despair, and when
you see that you cannot bear it anymore, draw back a
little and have a cup of tea.*

—Elder Sophrony of Essex

A S A TEA DRINKER, I can certainly appreciate this
quote. Being a wife and mother, I can appreciate it
even more. I have stood at the brink of the abyss of despair.
I'm sure you can recognize the look on the faces of those
who have been there if you take a moment. A face with eyebrows knit together, indicating one more step will push that
person over the edge.

When we find ourselves at the abyss, we do not want

to take tea at the very edge of the cliff, but, as Elder Soph-rony says, "draw back a little." But how does one accomplish this when you go to bed later than planned because the eighteen-year-old got home late, and the baby wakes up an hour later demanding attention, and you know it's only a few short hours before your own personal tornado (the eight-year-old) sounds the alarm to announce his arrival to the morning? How do you stay in the present when a school holiday is coming up and you know the personalities min-gling together throughout the day are more likely to prove explosive than enjoyable? Or what if you are dreading each phone call because of financial trouble, or you are trudging through a deep, dark moment in your life? What then?

My mother reminds me often that tea has a way of keeping you in the moment. It's not like coffee, which, in our society, is meant to keep you always moving forward. Tea encourages the partaker to sit down and rest a moment. It is a sort of reset button for the weary. If we push ourselves beyond what we can bear for the sake of being strong, we will fall over, teacup and all, and find that staring up from the darkness of the abyss is far more terrifying than standing at the brink.

Let us step back and take tea together as mothers. Of course we may not be able to sit at each other's tables and sip a perfectly steeped pot together, but we can pray for one another and be an encouragement. We can make a pot of gratitude for all the Lord has blessed us with and sip it throughout the day through prayer and the reading of His Word. We can choose to face the difficulties, in the strength of Christ our Lord, and lay down the idea that we must somehow bear it all. How freeing is that thought alone?

May we take hold of even the smallest moments each day to enter into prayer, allowing us to step back and drink in Christ, for He promises to quench our thirst and give us His peace. Thank God!

ADDICTION

The following prayers are excerpted and adapted from the Akathist Hymn to the Theotokos, the Inexhaustible Cup, available from St. Paisius Monastery (used by permission).

Prayer I ॐ

O our merciful and holy Lady Theotokos, hope and refuge of the orphan, defense of the stranger, help of those in need, and protection of those who are bitter: you see our misfortune, you see our sorrow. From all sides, we are assailed by temptations, and there is no one to protect us. Help us, for we are weak. Feed us, for we are strangers. Show us the way, for we are lost. Heal us, for we hurt. Save us, for there is no hope for us. We have no other recourse, neither protection nor consolation, but you, O Mother of all who suffer and are burdened. Look down upon us sinners who are harsh and bitter, and protect us by your holy veil, that we may be delivered from all evil that assails us, and especially from drunkenness, so that we may always glorify your all-holy name. Amen.

Prayer II ⌁

O all-merciful sovereign Lady, we come to your protection. Do not despise our petitions, but kindly hear us—wives, children, husbands, parents, and all those who suffer from heavy affliction of addictions of all sorts—and restore those who, because of it, fall away from our holy Mother the Church and its salvation. O merciful Theotokos, touch their hearts and speedily restore them from their fallen state, and lead them to salutary repentance. Implore your Son, Christ our God, to forgive us our trespasses and not to turn away His mercies from His people, but that He would strengthen us in sobriety and chastity. Accept, O all-holy Theotokos, the petitions of mothers shedding tears about their children, wives sobbing for their husbands, children, orphans, beggars, and all those who were forsaken, and all of us who venerate your icon, and let your prayers carry our petitions to the throne of the Almighty. Cover us and keep us from all snares of the enemy and the traps of the evil one, and at the dreadful hour of our death, help us to pass the ordeal without stumbling. By your prayers, save us from eternal condemnation so that God's mercy may cover us for the ages to come. Amen.

Troparion in Tone IV ⌁

Today we faithful come to the divine and miraculous icon of the Most Holy Theotokos, who fills the faithful from the inexhaustible cup of her mercy and shows them great miracles; and we who have seen them and heard of them rejoice in our heart and cry out, with deep feeling and devotion, O all-merciful sovereign Lady, heal our ills and our passions by praying to your Son, Christ our God, that He may save our souls!

ANGER

> *The first step toward freedom from anger is to keep the lips silent when the heart is stirred; the next, to keep thoughts silent when the soul is upset; the last, to be totally calm when unclean winds are blowing.*
> *(St. John Climacus)*

Now, how can we possibly do this as mothers? "The first step toward freedom from anger is to keep the lips silent when the heart is stirred." All too often I go wherever the "stirring" of the heart might lead me. I react instead of respond to the situation, and I have no thought for the heart issue we're facing, but instead look for the nearest emotional "bandaid" so we can fix it and move on. What would happen if I kept my lips silent? First of all, I think my children might get worried that something was wrong with me, but after the shock wore off, I think it would allow them the opportunity to think and to see that Mom is taking the situation seriously enough to put some thought into her words.

"The next, to keep thoughts silent when the soul is upset." How wild are the minds of mothers! I know my

mind is quick to assume the role of god instead of seeking
the will of Christ our Lord. My own thoughts become judge
and jury when an offense has been committed. And if my
mind is busy with its own thoughts, how on earth can my
ears listen to the evidence or my eyes take in the attitude
visible on my child's face or in her body language? But if I
did silence my mind—if I did put up road blocks to stop
the constant traffic—how would my response differ? Those
times I have stepped back and taken a moment in silence,
I have found many of the issues I thought were so press-
ing actually fall away to reveal heart issues—issues I need to
bring before the Lord in continual prayers. Of course this
doesn't mean discipline may not be in order, but I will not
be sinning in my anger if I take that moment to reflect, pray
for my child, and address him in love. What impact might
I have on my children's souls if I consistently approached
them in this manner?

I have a friend who made a pact with a group of young
moms long ago that they would treat their children, all the
time, as they do in public. What an amazing idea. I know I
don't intentionally speak to them differently at home, but
often I do. You know how you can be—uh—speaking loudly
to your children, and then the phone rings. What happens?
Ask them, they know. Your voice changes to that fairy-
godmother-sounding sweet voice. What would happen if
they received that voice all the time?

Yes, when we're interacting with other people, it's like running a sprint. It's easier to keep it together, even if you get frustrated, when it's short-term. Interacting with your children and family—well, that's a marathon. I think we often try to sprint through our marathon of parenting, and when we do that it's impossible to maintain the positive pace for very long. If we run the mommy marathon like a marathon, we will pace ourselves, take "water" breaks along the way, and have more reasonable expectations for the length of the journey.

"The last, to be totally calm when unclean winds are blowing." What does that mean exactly? I'll give my mommy guess. It could mean that when storms come, in this case family storms, we should aspire to be calm however hard the winds blow, anchoring ourselves in Christ. What an impact this could have on our homes.

O Lord of hosts, hear my prayer. Lead me to walk Your path in silence and avoid the snare of anger. Bring me to those still waters and calm my heart and my mind so I may then address not only the actions of my child, but more importantly, the heart of my child. As You deal with me, O merciful Lord, may I also deal with this child You have placed in my care. Amen.

> *As with the appearance of light, darkness retreats; so,*
> *at the fragrance of humility, all anger and bitterness*
> *vanishes. (St. John Climacus)*

O Lord and Master of my life, have mercy on me, a sinner, and grant me Your strength and Your humility that all anger and bitterness may vanish from my heart. Grant me the courage to walk in Your ways. Amen.

Dear Lord, shine a light on this sin of anger plaguing my child. Let him/her learn from each conflict how to be present with You and seek to imitate Your forgiveness, as You forgave those who persecuted You. Amen.

> *"Be angry, and do not sin": do not let the sun go down on*
> *your wrath, nor give place to the devil. (Eph. 4:26–27)*

Dear Lord, grant me the strength to lay down anger and put on compassion instead. Your love for this child is greater than mine, and You are able to see the whole picture while I am limited by my humanity. Teach me to love this child in the same way You offer Your love to all mankind. For You are holy, now and ever and unto ages of ages. Amen.

> *Anger is tamed and becomes transformed into benevolence*
> *only through courage and mercy. (St. Gregory of Sinai)*

As You have made me, Your lowly servant, in Your image, now also transform my heart and mind so that every bit of influence I have over my children will direct them to Your good and perfect ways. Let me be always conscious of my own fallen state so that I will have an abundance of mercy for my children. May my words and actions be a method of showing them Your holiness, and may my shortcomings not cause them to stumble. May I repent openly about my failings, and in all humility let me take up the glorious cross of motherhood and admonish my children in a way that is just before You. Remind me in every moment of frustration toward my children to stop and seek Your will for each situation. Help me not to *react* to offenses, but instead to *act* in love, that they may know I am a servant of the King. In the name of the Father and the Son and the Holy Spirit. Amen.

> *Are you angry? Be angry at your sins, beat your soul, afflict your conscience, be strict in judgment and a terrible punisher of your own sins. This is the benefit of anger, wherefore God placed it in us. (St. John Chrysostom)*

ANXIETY*

> *Be anxious for nothing, but in everything by prayer and supplication, with thanksgiving, let your requests be made known to God; and the peace of God, which surpasses all understanding, will guard your hearts and minds through Christ Jesus. Finally, brethren, whatever things are true, whatever things are noble, whatever things are just, whatever things are pure, whatever things are lovely, whatever things are of good report, if there is any virtue and if there is anything praiseworthy—meditate on these things. (Phil. 4:6—8)*

O Lord of hosts, calm my anxious heart. In Your love and concern for the salvation of my soul, bring to mind Your loving-kindness and grant me Your strength to block out every thought or feeling that does not bring glory to You. Teach me to keep

---

*   If you are consistently struggling with anxiety or depression, dear mama, seek the help of a medical professional and your priest.

my mind in the present that I may meditate upon Your goodness whenever I am assaulted by anxious thoughts. If I may not
be freed from the anxiety plaguing me, let me continue to work
out my salvation, and allow me to know Your peace and trust
You for each step heavenward. Amen.

> *Do not despair! The Lord is near. Declare to Him all*
> *of our sorrows and confusion. When human means*
> *are insufficient for understanding, then God's help*
> *immediately grants beneficial thoughts, when we turn*
> *to Him as children to a father. (St. Moses)*

Dear Lord, have mercy on me. My thoughts seem unyielding,
but I know You are more powerful. Thank You that You have
not given me a spirit of fear, but of power, of love, and of a
sound mind. Help me not to despair but to draw closer to You.
Let me not forget the challenges of this world are great, but
You are greater still. For You are holy, now and ever and unto
ages of ages. Amen.

> *You shall not be afraid of the terror by night,*
> *Nor of the arrow that flies by day,*
> *Nor of the pestilence that walks in darkness,*
> *Nor of the destruction that lays waste at noonday.*
>
> *A thousand may fall at your side,*
> *And ten thousand at your right hand;*
> *But it shall not come near you.*
> *Only with your eyes shall you look,*
> *And see the reward of the wicked.*
>
> *Because you have made the Lord, who is my refuge,*
> *Even the Most High, your dwelling place,*

> *No evil shall befall you,*
> *Nor shall any plague come near your dwelling;*
> *For He shall give His angels charge over you,*
> *To keep you in all your ways.*
> *In their hands they shall bear you up,*
> *Lest you dash your foot against a stone.*
> > (Ps. 91:5–12)

O holy guardian angel, sent from the Lord of hosts for our protection, stand guard over my children as they sleep that they may not be afraid. Speak the truth of our Master's words into their ears that they may not forget His goodness and His protection. Pray for them and guide them in His ways. Amen.

> *No matter how many waves rise up in your soul,*
> *always flee to Christ. The Savior will come to help*
> *and will calm the waves. Believe that the Lord has*
> *providentially arranged your life for our healing; do*
> *not reject it and do not seek bodily rest and imagined*
> *peace. It is necessary rather to be shaken and endure*
> *much. (St. Leo)*

ARGUING

> *But avoid foolish and ignorant disputes, knowing that*
> *they generate strife. And a servant of the Lord must*
> *not quarrel but be gentle to all, able to teach, patient,*
> *in humility correcting those who are in opposition, if*
> *God perhaps will grant them repentance, so that they*
> *may know the truth, and that they may come to their*
> *senses and escape the snare of the devil, having been*
> *taken captive by him to do his will. (2 Tim. 2:23–26)*

Lord God, help me not to enter into arguments with my children, but let me be calm and humble as I correct their errors. It is so hard, Lord, to hold my tongue when my children argue. Allow me to see the eternal picture and use my words sparingly, and only in ways that will be beneficial for their godly training and for the salvation of their souls. Amen.

> *Once we have entrusted our hope about something to*
> *God, we no longer quarrel with our neighbor over it.*
> *(St. Kosmas Aitolos)*

O Lord, who spoke the world into existence, now allow Your words to speak life to others through me. Keep me ever aware of my words and interactions with my neighbors and my children, and show me in each situation how to entrust my hope to You. For You are blessed always, now and unto ages of ages. Amen.

> *Do all things without complaining and disputing, that*
> *you may become blameless and harmless, children of*
> *God without fault in the midst of a crooked and per-*
> *verse generation, among whom you shine as lights in*
> *the world, holding fast the word of life, so that I may*
> *rejoice in the day of Christ that I have not run in vain*
> *or labored in vain. (Phil. 2:14–16)*

Blessed Lord Jesus, my child is facing many challenges in this "crooked and perverse generation." Grant him/her the courage to stand firm in the faith and be a light to others, speaking the truth in love and remaining silent when words would benefit no one. Help him/her to avoid entering into arguments, but instead let him/her handle each challenge with humility. Let him/her know Your peace when he/she chooses to hold his/her tongue in the face of adversity. Amen.

COMPLAINING

> *The Lord bears all the weaknesses of men, but He does not bear a man who is always murmuring and does not leave him without chastisement. (St. Isaac the Syrian)*

Lord Jesus Christ, let every word that comes from my mouth be acceptable in Your sight and full of Your praises. Remind me when I feel like complaining that our Lord Jesus Christ endured the very Cross without a single complaint. Let my mouth speak of Your goodness, and may I tell the world of my great joy because of Your finished work on the Cross. When the worm of complaint tries to penetrate my heart and mind, let it be a reminder to me to pray for my family and those in need. Amen.

> *If you suffer some misfortune, then think: "The Lord sees my heart, and if it pleases Him, it will be well both for me and for others." And thus your soul will always be at peace. But if someone murmurs, "This is bad, and that is bad," then he will never have peace in his soul, even though he fasts and prays a lot. (St. Silouan the Athonite)*

O Holy Trinity, bless my children and bring to their minds all there is to be thankful for—the Cross, the grave, and the third-day Resurrection. Let every praise that has been sung or chanted in Your holy temple come to mind and allow their young souls to find contentment in You. In the name of the Father and of the Son and of the Holy Spirit. Amen.

CORRECTION/CHASTISEMENT

*The will of the parents should be imprinted upon each
step—of course in a general way. Without this, the
behavior of the child can easily become corrupted.
(St. Theophan the Recluse)*

All-Holy Trinity, have mercy on me as I endeavor to bring up my children in Your righteousness. Let me not forget the importance of their spiritual instruction, and grant me the wisdom to help my children to walk in Your ways. Grant me understanding that my correction may be just and done with kindness and love. At times I grow weary, O Lord, of the consistent effort required to train my children. Grant me the strength to accept each trial with joy and the ability to discern the best way to address each challenge for each child. Amen.

*Now no chastening seems to be joyful for the present,
but painful; nevertheless, afterward it yields the
peaceable fruit of righteousness to those who have been
trained by it. (Heb. 12:11)*

Dear Father, You have made me a mother to my children and appointed me to train and correct them in their youth. Allow my children to see the benefit of their correction, that resentment and bitterness may not grow in their hearts. Let me not forget how You, in Your love, chastise Your children. Let me, in like manner, correct my children that they may acquire the "peaceable fruit of righteousness." For You are holy, now and ever and unto ages of ages. Amen.

> *We are so concerned with our children's schooling [and worldly success]; if only we were equally zealous in bringing them up in the discipline and instruction of the Lord. . . . This, then, is our task: to educate both ourselves and our children in godliness; otherwise what answer will we have before Christ's judgment seat?*
> *(St. John Chrysostom)*

DEMONIC INFLUENCE

> *Therefore submit to God. Resist the devil and he will flee from you. Draw near to God and He will draw near to you. Cleanse your hands, you sinners; and purify your hearts, you double-minded. Lament and mourn and weep! Let your laughter be turned to mourning and your joy to gloom. Humble yourselves in the sight of the Lord, and He will lift you up.*
> *(James 4:7–10)*

Almighty God, who delivered Your people from the bondage of the adversary, and through Your Son cast down Satan like lightning, deliver *(Name)* also from every influence of unclean spirits. Command Satan to depart far from *(Name)* by the power of Your only-begotten Son. Rescue him/her from demonic imaginings and darkness. Fill him/her with the light of the Holy Spirit that he/she may be guarded against all snares of crafty demons. Grant that an angel will always go before *(Name)* and lead him/her to the path of righteousness all the days of his/her life, to the honor of Your glorious Name, Father, Son, and Holy Spirit, now and forever. Amen.

> *Our chief enemies are the demons who fight to conquer us through our passions. The most powerful weapon against all their evil machinations, snares, and arrows is humility. They are the creatures of pride and are able to conquer those who proudly think that they can do battle with them. (St. Macarius)*

Dearest Lord Jesus, You whom demons fear, provide protection for Your servant (*Name*) against the wiles of the enemy. Let the enemy be vanquished by his/her humility and complete confidence in Your power and Your work on the Cross, which conquered sin and death. Deliver (*Name*) from any unholy influence. Amen.

DEPRESSION*

✛ ✛ ✛ ✛ ✛ ✛ ✛ ✛ ✛ ✛ ✛ ✛

The New Martyr St. Maria of Gatchina

Commemorated on January 26

The small town of Gatchina, in Russia, was home to the New Martyr Saint Maria. Many people suffering from depression, grief, and despair would come to visit this blessed nun because the Lord had seen fit to grant her the gift of consoling those who sorrowed. She herself had suffered much, having been stricken with encephalitis and later Parkinson's disease, which caused her to become immobile and severely affected her speech. Though this disease

---

* If you are consistently struggling with anxiety or depression, dear mama, seek the help of a medical professional and your priest.

was usually accompanied by unpredictable moodiness and depression, Saint Maria remained meek and kind and spent her time in constant prayer. Those suffering from depression seek prayers from this righteous saint.

Troparion (Tone 4)
> O our blessed Mother Maria,
> who bore the cross of illness so meekly and humbly,
> with such sobriety and prayer that God granted you the gift
> of consolation:
> Pray for us sinners who know not how to repent, that God
> may grant us His great mercy.[3]

✠　✠　✠　✠　✠　✠　✠　✠　✠　✠　✠　✠

Heavenly Father, I feel cast down and pressed on every side. Be a light to my darkened path and lift my head above the waters of despair that threaten to pull me under. Grant me the courage to seek the help I need and the strength to bring myself to Your holy hospital, the Church. Take my hand, O Lord my God, as you took the hand of Peter when he cried out to You in his despair. Lift me up with Your mighty right hand that I may walk in Your strength and victory. Allow me to stand on Your feet and take each step with You as a little child. Let me cling to Your robes that I may not fall into darkness. For You are holy, now and ever and unto ages of ages. Amen.

> *We are hard-pressed on every side, yet not crushed;*
> *we are perplexed, but not in despair; persecuted, but*
> *not forsaken; struck down, but not destroyed—always*
> *carrying about in the body the dying of the Lord Jesus,*
> *that the life of Jesus also may be manifested in our*
> *body. (2 Cor. 4:8–10)*

All seems dark, O Lord, yet I cry out to You with the little faith I can muster. Lead me safely through the dark shadows. Help me to know I am protected and need not fear. Remind me at every moment that You have not abandoned me, but that the path You have marked for me is secure, and by Your power my foot will not slip on the narrow path. Let me know Your peace that passes all understanding and train my mind to dwell on those things that allow Your light to shine upon my soul. In the name of the Father and the Son and the Holy Spirit. Amen.

> *The weather shifts from cloudy to clear and then back to rain; thus it is with human nature. One must always expect clouds to hide the sun sometimes. Even the saints have had their dark hours, days and weeks. They say then that "God has left them" in order that they may know truly how utterly wretched they are of themselves, without His support. These times of darkness, when all seems meaningless, ridiculous and vain, when one is beset by doubt and temptations, are inevitable. But even these times can be harvested for good. (The Way of the Ascetic, p. 84)*

O Christ our God, who suffer the little children to come unto You, bring protection and comfort to my child suffering from depression. Take from him/her this distress and grant clear direction for how to address this ailment. Amen.

> *Prayer is a remedy against grief and depression. (Abba Nilus)*

Holy Mother of God, be my mother and place a hedge of protection around my heart, my mind, and my mouth that I may not sin against your Son. Protect me, O holy lady, from the sorrows of this life and pray that I will trust your Son and Savior at every moment of every day. Let me imitate you and stand boldly at the feet of Christ as you did at His crucifixion. Remind me always to run to His tomb and proclaim His Resurrection that the demons may be afraid and leave His lowly servant in peace. For you are blessed among women and mother to all Christians. Amen.

DIFFICULT PREGNANCY

> *For You formed my inward parts;*
> *You covered me in my mother's womb.*
> *I will praise You, for I am fearfully and wonderfully*
> *   made;*
> *Marvelous are Your works,*
> *And that my soul knows very well.*
> *My frame was not hidden from You,*
> *When I was made in secret,*
> *And skillfully wrought in the lowest parts of the earth*
> *Your eyes saw my substance, being yet unformed.*
> *And in Your book they all were written,*
> *The days fashioned for me,*
> *When as yet there were none of them. (Ps. 139:13–16)*

O Lord God Almighty, Creator of all things and Giver of knowledge to mankind, who fashioned the body of man from the earth and breathed into his nostrils the breath of life, granting him Your blessings that he might increase and multiply by means of the birth of children: I fervently entreat You who love mankind to bless me, Your servant, who am with child, granting me help and comfort at this trying time. Ease my labor and bring me to a safe delivery. O Lord, open the treasury of Your mercies and Your compassion to me, and let me give birth to a fruitful vine to be a cause of joy to me all the days of my life. For You are blessed, together with Your Only-begotten Son, and Your most-holy, good and life-creating Spirit, now and ever and unto ages of ages. Amen.[4]

DISOBEDIENCE

> *Children, obey your parents in all things, for this is well pleasing to the Lord. Fathers, do not provoke your children, lest they become discouraged. Bondservants, obey in all things your masters according to the flesh, not with eye service, as men-pleasers, but in sincerity of heart, fearing God. And whatever you do, do it heartily, as to the Lord and not to men, knowing that from the Lord you will receive the reward of the inheritance; for you serve the Lord Christ. (Col. 3:20–24)*

Holy Lord Jesus, our righteous loving Father who desires obedience more than sacrifice, help me to be a trustworthy example to my children in my obedience to You, and keep me from provoking them "lest they become discouraged." Show me, O Lord, my shortcomings that I may gently correct my children and participate in turning their hearts toward You. Give me the strength to obey You in all things with joy. May I not desire to control my children, but rather direct them to willingly place themselves in Your service. Amen.

> *Genuine obedience which brings great benefit to the soul comes when you act in defiance of yourself. Then the Lord Himself takes you in His arms and blesses your labors. (St. Nikon)*

O Holy Spirit, fill me with Your love, joy, peace, longsuffering, kindness, goodness, faithfulness, gentleness, self-control, and mercy as I train my children to be obedient to me, and more importantly to You. Instruct me in denying my own will that I may walk in obedience. I confess I rely on my own mind and my own understanding often and attempt to train my children in my own strength. Forgive me and be a bright light to my path. Take me by the hand and lead me to walk in humility so my service to You may benefit my children. Amen.

> *Therefore, my beloved, as you have always obeyed, not as in my presence only, but now much more in my absence, work out your own salvation with fear and trembling; for it is God who works in you both to will and to do for His good pleasure. (Phil. 2:12–13)*

Lord Jesus, You alone know the heart of my child; help him/her to resist the temptation to obey only when a parent is watching. Remind him/her that You are a loving God who sees everything done in secret. Amen.

> *By obedience a man is guarded against pride. Prayer is given for the sake of obedience. The grace of the Holy Spirit is also given for obedience. This is why obedience is higher than prayer and fasting. (St. Silouan the Athonite)*

ENEMIES

> *Whoever will not love his enemies cannot know the Lord and the sweetness of the Holy Spirit. The Holy Spirit teaches us to love our enemies in such a way that*

> *we pity their souls as if they were our own children.*
> *(St. Silouan the Athonite)*

Teach me, O Lord of hosts, to love my enemies as You love all mankind, who are undeserving of Your love. Remind me that my enemies are made in Your image and likeness, and if I despise them I despise You also. Soften my heart toward those who persecute me and grant me Your strength to pray for them that they may know Your goodness. Amen.

> *When you have been insulted, cursed, or persecuted*
> *by someone, do not think of what has happened to you,*
> *but of what will come from it, and you will see that*
> *your insulter has become the cause of many benefits to*
> *you, not only in this age, but in that which is to come.*
> *(St. Mark the Ascetic)*

When You were scourged, O Lord, and beaten and spat upon, You did not curse those who cursed You. When they pulled out Your beard and placed the crown of thorns on Your head and mocked You, You did not speak a word against them. When they placed Your holy body on the cross, even then You asked Your Father in heaven to forgive them. Change my heart, O God, that I too may have compassion on my enemies. Let me love them the way You love them. For You are blessed now and ever and unto ages of ages. Amen.

> *I ask you to try something. If someone grieves you, or*
> *dishonors you, or takes something of yours, then pray*
> *like this: "Lord, we are all Your creatures. Pity Your*
> *servants, and turn them to repentance," and then you*
> *will perceptibly bear grace in your soul. Induce your*
> *heart to love your enemies, and the Lord, seeing your*
> *good will, shall help you in all things, and will Himself*

> *show you experience. But whoever thinks evil of his*
> *enemies does not have love for God and has not known*
> *God. (St. Silouan the Athonite)*

Dear Lord, please turn the heart of anger my child has toward his/her enemies and teach him/her to love those You love, whether they deserve it or not. Let them see Your image in each face and grant them compassion and love toward all mankind. In the name of the Father and the Son and the Holy Spirit. Amen.

ENVY

By Your hand, O Lord, I was fearfully and wonderfully made. Help me to accept the talents You have given me and to use them, with joy, as an example to my children and as an offering of thanksgiving to You. Let me not envy those who have different gifts and abilities but be thankful for my function within the body of Christ. Remind me that You created us to work as a body. If You have made me as an ear, let me not envy the function of the eye but rejoice in what You have purposed me to do, and let me do it with all my might. Amen.

> *Love suffers long and is kind; love does not envy; love*
> *does not parade itself, is not puffed up; does not behave*
> *rudely, does not seek its own, is not provoked, thinks*
> *no evil; does not rejoice in iniquity, but rejoices in the*
> *truth; bears all things, believes all things, hopes all*
> *things, endures all things. (1 Cor. 13:4–7)*

Creator of heaven and earth and Master of my soul, protect my heart from envy and show me instead how to be content in every situation. Let not my mind dwell on earthly things, which will all pass away, but on storing up treasures in heaven. May my hands remain open to accept Your blessings and to joyfully give to those in need. In the name of the Father and the Son and the Holy Spirit. Amen.

> *What torments an envious person? The good fortune or preference of a neighbor; although he himself has the same fortune and at times is also given preference, it is annoying to him that his neighbor has these. But where there is love and humility, all nuances of envy are burned up.* (St. Macarius)

Dear Lord Jesus, help my child to rejoice when good things happen to others instead of being envious. Let him/her accept with joy what he/she has been given and give freely of possessions and goodwill toward all mankind. Teach him/her to embrace Your humility and avoid every kind of envious thought. For You are blessed unto ages of ages. Amen.

> *In the beginning, envy is revealed through inappropriate zeal and rivalry, and later by fervor with spite and the blaming of the one who is envied.* (St. Ambrose)

O Christ my God, my child is envious of things his/her siblings receive, refusing to be comforted and desiring not to work harder but rather to have gifts he/she has not earned. Touch his/her heart, O Lord, that he/she will be joyful for the accomplishments of others and that he/she will be challenged to work hard, in all humility, to desire Your favor above all things. Amen.

FEELING OF FAILURE AS A PARENT

> *Understand two thoughts, and fear them. One says,*
> *"You are a saint," the other, "You won't be saved."*
> *Both of these thoughts are from the enemy, and there*
> *is no truth in them. But think this way: I am a great*
> *sinner, but the Lord is merciful. He loves people very*
> *much, and He will forgive my sins. (St. Silouan the*
> *Athonite)*

O Holy Trinity, I come before You as the Publican acknowledging my unworthiness of Your grace and mercy toward Your lowly servant. And while I feel my shortcomings are great, I humble myself before Your throne and ask that You bestow Your grace and mercy and grant me the courage to walk in Your ways. For You are my God, and to You I ascribe glory and honor, in the name of the Father and the Son and the Holy Spirit, now and ever and unto ages of ages. Amen.

> *Many are they who say of me,*
> *"There is no help for him in God." Selah*
>
> *But You, O Lord, are a shield for me,*
> *My glory and the One who lifts up my head.*
> *I cried to the Lord with my voice,*
> *And He heard me from His holy hill. (Ps. 3:2—4)*

I have fallen, as a parent, and can only stand if You, in Your mercy, give me the strength to stand. Thank You that You hear the prayer of the sinner and freely forgive. Accept my confession and help me to receive Your forgiveness so I may move forward with joy. Show me Your will that I may follow and let my actions reveal my repentant heart. Amen.

*Even if all spiritual fathers, patriarchs, hierarchs, and
all the people forgive you, you are unforgiven if you
don't repent in action. (St. Kosmas Aitolos)*

Dearest Lord Jesus, show me how to be a loving mother to
my children. You know the desire of my heart is to mother
my children in a way that will draw them to You. Forgive my
shortcomings and help me not to sink into despair, but to rise
up in faith with the knowledge that Your holy power is strong
enough to sustain me and guide me to be the mother my children need. Help me to be slow to speak, quick to listen, and
quick to forgive my children of their faults. Grant me Your
vision for my children that I may know how to train, encourage, and pray for them. For You are holy, now and ever and
unto ages of ages. Amen.

FINANCIAL STRAIN

*"Therefore do not worry, saying, 'What shall we eat?'
or 'What shall we drink?' or 'What shall we wear?'
For after all these things the Gentiles seek. For your
heavenly Father knows that you need all these things.
But seek first the kingdom of God and His righteousness, and all these things shall be added to you. Therefore do not worry about tomorrow, for tomorrow will
worry about its own things. Sufficient for the day is its
own trouble." (Matt. 6:31–34)*

I am thankful, dear Lord, that I can trust You with the financial strain I am facing right now. I trust Your faithfulness and
believe that You will not forget Your humble servant in her distress. Thank You for the constant reminder, even from nature,

of how You provide for all You have created, and how much more I can be assured that You will provide what is necessary for the salvation of my soul. Amen.

> *If you begin to guard wealth, it will not be yours.*
> *But if you begin to distribute it, you will not lose it.*
> *(St. Basil the Great)*

All that I have is Yours; lead me away from believing anything different. Let me strive to serve You on this earth with everything I possess. Allow my example of faith to build up my children in right faith that will remain with them all the days of their lives. Help me not to be afraid to give freely to those in greater need than myself; rather grant me a joyful heart as You provide ways to serve others. For You are holy, now and ever and unto ages of ages. Amen.

> *Some suffer much from poverty and sickness, but are*
> *not humbled, and so they suffer without profit. But*
> *one who is humbled will be happy in all circumstances,*
> *because the Lord is his riches and joy, and all people*
> *will wonder at the beauty of his soul. (St. Silouan the*
> *Athonite)*

O Lord, have mercy on me, a sinner. Forgive me when I have been angry or in despair when it seems there just won't be enough. I choose to trust You and accept what You provide as what is important for my soul. When I can't see the way out, help me to turn to You as the light unto my path. If You provide wealth, let me accept it with humility and be a good steward in thanksgiving. If You allow poverty, let me rejoice in Your goodness despite my financial situation. For You are my

everlasting treasure, and to You I ascribe glory, to the Father
and the Son and the Holy Spirit. Amen.

> *It is a mistake to think that wealth or abundance or*
> *even sufficient means would be beneficial or reassur-*
> *ing. The rich worry even more than the poor and*
> *impoverished. Poverty and being in want are closer to*
> *humility and to salvation if only the one who is poor*
> *does not become fainthearted, but with faith and hope*
> *relies on the all-good Providence of God. Until this day*
> *the Lord has fed us, and He has the power to do so in*
> *the future. (St. Ambrose)*

GREED/SELFISHNESS

> *All things are lawful for me, but not all things are*
> *helpful; all things are lawful for me, but not all things*
> *edify. Let no one seek his own, but each one the other's*
> *well-being. (1 Cor. 10:23–24)*

Dear Lord, bless my child who is struggling with selfishness.
Let my life be an example of joyfully giving of myself and my
possessions for Your glory. If my example has caused my little one to stumble, show me my own sin that I may repent
and start anew. Teach me, O Lord, to instruct my child in Your
ways with patience and compassion that he/she may find joy in
giving. Amen.

> *Every individual instinctively strives for happiness.*
> *This desire has been implanted in our nature by the*
> *Creator Himself, and therefore it is not sinful. But*
> *it is important to understand that in this temporary*
> *life it is impossible to find full happiness, because that*
> *comes from God and cannot be attained without Him.*

> *Only He, who is the ultimate Good and the Source*
> *of All Good, can quench our thirst for happiness.*
> *(St. Innocent of Alaska)*

Grant, O Lord, Your wisdom to teach my children to be lovers of God rather than lovers of the world. In their innocence let me not neglect these great lessons necessary for their souls. If my heart has forgotten these lessons, or wasn't properly taught, forgive me and help me to learn in all humility. Help us to accept the gifts you provide for us, but let us also be eager to give whatever we have to those in need. Remind us always that this world is our temporary home, a mere shadow of the glories to come. In the name of the Father and the Son and the Holy Spirit. Amen.

> *"Whoever desires to come after Me, let him deny him-*
> *self, and take up his cross, and follow Me. For whoever*
> *desires to save his life will lose it, but whoever loses his*
> *life for My sake and the gospel's will save it. For what*
> *will it profit a man if he gains the whole world, and*
> *loses his own soul?" (Matt. 8:34–36)*

HOMOSEXUALITY & SEXUAL IMMORALITY

> *All passions are dishonorable, for the soul is even more*
> *prejudiced and degraded by sin than is the body by dis-*
> *ease; but the worst of all passions is lust between men.*
> *. . . There is nothing, absolutely nothing more mad or*
> *damaging than this perversity. (St. John Chrysostom)*

This world is embracing homosexuality and all manner of sexual sin as virtue, and my children are constantly bombarded by the lies of the enemy. Forgive me if I have, by word or action, suggested that sexual sin is acceptable in Your sight. Protect them, O Lord, from the influence of sexual sin. Help them to be fully aware of the cunning ways of the enemy, and grant them the strength to cling to Your truth and embrace Your righteousness and holy love. Amen.

> *Do you not know that the unrighteous will not inherit the kingdom of God? Do not be deceived. Neither fornicators, nor idolaters, nor adulterers, nor homosexuals, nor sodomites, nor thieves, nor covetous, nor drunkards, nor revilers, nor extortioners will inherit the kingdom of God. (1 Cor. 6:9–10)*

You created us, O Lord. Male and female You created us. Have mercy on my child who is being tempted to participate in sexual sin. Open his/her eyes to Your truth that he/she may walk in Your ways with clarity of heart and mind. Help me not forget to teach him/her about Your right and good plan for sexual intimacy, which is between a man and a woman within the Holy Sacrament of Marriage. Let him/her desire to preserve his/her sexual purity. When he/she is tempted, let Your "way of escape" be known to him/her. Help me be available to my child for compassionate guidance and as a fierce ally to fight against the wicked schemes of the enemy.

> *Peace is promised to us in the future life, but here on earth—labor and temptation. Blessed is the man that endures temptation (James 1:12) (St. Moses)*

Dear Lord Jesus, my child has participated in homosexual behavior. Help me to stand firm in the faith, calling that which is sin sinful. Help my heart to be open to this precious child You have given me, and guide me so that I may bring him/her up in the "training and admonition of the Lord" (Eph. 6:4). Bring my child to repentance and healing through Your loving kindness that his/her soul may see Your salvation. For You are blessed now and ever and unto ages of ages. Amen.

Our Father, Your Word tells us the "unrighteous will not inherit the kingdom of God" (1 Cor. 6:9), including those committing sexual sin. But You also tell us of Your boundless mercy. Draw my child unto Yourself, O Lord, that he/she may desire forgiveness and change his/her ways to bring glory to Your image, present within him/her, through the care of his/her body, as the temple You have created it to be. Help me to show Your unconditional love and in all humility speak Your truth. In the name of the Father and the Son and the Holy Spirit. Amen.

> *Everyone who even thinks about entering the right path is liable to endure a multitude of all possible temptations. Blessed and most blessed are those who have entered the right path.* (St. Macarius)

IDLE TALK/GOSSIP

> *Salvation is not gained when we speak idly or when we pass through our days without consideration. Be attentive to your tongue and to your mind, for the guarding of these fills the soul with the light of God. But that one whose mouth is unbridled stores up various impurities in his soul.* (Elder Ephraim of Philotheou)

Throughout Great Lent we call upon You to "Set a guard, O Lord, over my mouth; Keep watch over the door of my lips" (Ps. 141:3). Dear Lord, hear my prayer. Help me not to justify my words but rather to use my words for Your glory and the edification of Your people. Let me not speak without care in front of others, in my home, or in my heart. For You are holy, now and ever and unto ages of ages. Amen.

> With it [the tongue] we bless our God and Father,
> and with it we curse men, who have been made in the
> similitude of God. Out of the same mouth proceed
> blessing and cursing. My brethren, these things ought
> not to be so. (James 3:9–10)

Your Word tells us, "Let the words of my mouth and the meditation of my heart be acceptable in Your sight, O Lord, my strength and my Redeemer" (Ps. 19:14). My child is struggling with the words of his/her mouth, speaking without concern for his/her neighbor. Help him/her to guard his/her mouth and make him/her aware of the power words can have to build up or tear down. As I endeavor to train my child in Your ways, let my words also be acceptable in Your sight. Amen.

INFERTILITY

> For You are my hope, O Lord God;
> You are my trust from my youth
> By You I have been upheld from birth;
> You are He who took me out of my mother's womb.
> My praise shall be continually of You.
>   (Ps. 75:5–6)

Dear Father in heaven, You know the desires of my heart, and You alone know what is necessary for my salvation. If it be Your will, grant me a child from my womb that I may raise my child to glorify Your name. If you choose not to open my womb to bear children, help my heart to stay open to whatever Your will may be. Thank You that I can put my complete trust in You. May I be obedient, giving thanks in all circumstances as I walk in Your goodness. Through the intercession of the Theotokos, O Savior, save us. Amen.

Prayer to Saint Anna, Mother of Mary ᘐ

O Holy Saint Anna, blessed grandmother of our Lord Jesus and mother of the Theotokos, pray for me. You desired a child and faithfully prayed that your womb would be fruitful, then willingly returned the fruit of your womb to the Lord's service that the world might be saved. Pray also for me, that I might not lose heart but in faith and prayer find comfort in the good and perfect will of our Father in heaven. Amen.

> But to Hannah he would give a double portion, for he loved Hannah, although the Lord had closed her womb.
> (1 Sam. 1:5)

Prayer to Saints Sarah, Rachel, and Hannah ᘐ

Holy Saints Sarah, Rachel, and Hannah, pray for me. You who know the longing a woman feels for a child, pray, if it be God's will, that my womb might also be fruitful. Pray I will not place my desire to have a child above my dedication to serve our God however He sees fit. Pray also that I may have patience and that my trust in the will of my Lord will not falter if He chooses to answer this prayer in another way. Amen.

IRRITABILITY

> As soon as you notice in yourself any irritation, just
> say firmly, "Lord have mercy." With prayer we are
> purified from every defilement. (St. Nektary)

Dear Jesus, help me, a sinner! I pray for Your mercy on my heart as I face each person and situation. You are merciful to me, unworthy though I am, and You provide the only peace that will truly calm my heart and mind. Come to my aid, O Lord, so that I will not lash out at those around me. Remind me in those moments that You, not I, are in control and that You, not I, have overcome the world. Grant me Your peace and quietness of mind that I may surrender my will to Yours and live my life for Your glory. Amen.

> You must make every effort to restrain yourself, so as
> not to acquire the unfortunate habit of losing your
> temper. This unbearable vice is not as noticeable in
> oneself as it is in others, and those who become angry
> over nothing are deserving of the fire of Gehenna.
> (St. Anthony)

O Holy Trinity, my child seems to be irritated with everyone and everything. Help me to know if, when, and how to correct my child during this time. Provide me with any insight that will help me to help him/her calm down and seek Your peace. Guide my words and actions, and help me not to try to control the situation but to submit it completely to You. For You are blessed, now and ever and unto ages of ages. Amen.

LAZINESS

> *Strive to struggle against laziness and drive it away and force yourself to labor in prayer. Remember that you must unfailingly force yourself in order to receive salvation. (St. Joseph)*

Dear Heavenly Father, I come to You in all honesty and ask Your forgiveness for the misuse of my time. I have complained about not being able to get things done, but I know I could have managed my time better. Help me to stay focused and seek Your help as I complete each task. May I find joy as the lowest in Your service, and let me see each task as a way to glorify You. Amen.

> *Laziness is not a small vice and it is numbered among the mortal sins, and therefore we must force ourselves to fulfill our duties and ask God for help and not rely on our own strength. Seeing our good intentions, He will give strength and power and will help us overcome the paralyzing laziness; but without our effort and good intention, God does not help. During time of infirmity and weakness let these take the place of our idleness: pain of heart, remorse, and humility. (St. Macarius)*

O my God and King, grant strength to Your servant *(Name)* to resist the temptation to be lazy. Let his/her perspective increase so that he/she may see the bigger picture and discern that even the smallest task is great in Your holy service. Help me to be an encouragement to him/her through instruction or prayer so that he/she may praise You with the works of his/her hands. In the Name of the Father and the Son and the Holy Spirit. Amen.

LYING

> These six things the LORD hates,
> Yes, seven are an abomination to Him:
> A proud look,
> A lying tongue,
> Hands that shed innocent blood,
> A heart that devises wicked plans,
> Feet that are swift in running to evil,
> A false witness who speaks lies,
> And one who sows discord among brethren.
>   (Prov. 6:16–19)

"Mercy and truth go before Your face" (Ps. 89:14), O Lord. Help my child to speak Your truth with boldness. Let him/her not deceive him/herself into believing a lie will be beneficial in any way. Guide his/her words that he/she may not sin against You. Free my child of the fears that may be behind temptations to lie, ever confident in Your love, which casts out fear. If I have influenced my child to lie by my own example, forgive me, dear Lord. Grant me the discernment to weed out my own sin and thus be able to guide the heart and tongue of my child. In the name of the Father and the Son and the Holy Spirit. Amen.

*Do not lie to one another, since you have put off the
old man with his deeds, and have put on the new man
who is renewed in knowledge according to the image of
Him who created him. (Col. 3:9–10)*

PERSECUTION

*Blessed are those who are persecuted for righteousness' sake,
For theirs is the kingdom of heaven. (Matt. 5:10)*

O Christ our God, who show mercy to the humble, who protect Your people with Your mighty right hand, protect my child suffering from persecutions. First I ask for deliverance for my child, but if this be not possible, I ask for heavenly strength that he/she may endure all persecution in humility and love, that Your name may be glorified. Grant me strength as a mother to encourage my child in his/her trial, always directing him/her heavenward, reminding him/her to keep his/her eye on the prize. As Your holy mother trusted in the will of God as she stood at the foot of Your Cross, let me also trust in Your will for my child. For You are a loving God, even in times of great persecution, and to You we ascribe glory, to the Father and the Son and the Holy Spirit, now and ever and unto ages of ages. Amen.

*If you want to serve God, prepare your heart not for
food, not for drink, not for rest, not for ease, but for
suffering, so that you may endure all temptations,
trouble and sorrow. Prepare for severities, fasts,*

spiritual struggles and many afflictions, for "by many
afflictions is it appointed to us to enter the Kingdom
of Heaven" (Acts 14:22); "The Heavenly Kingdom is
taken by force, and they who use force seize it" (Matt
11:12). (St. Sergius of Radonezh)

You tell us, O Lord, to take up our cross and follow You. You tell us that in this life there will be sorrow. You tell us not to be afraid of those who can kill the body but not the soul, but rather to fear the One who can destroy both body and soul in hell. You tell us not to fear the very devil, but to trust in You. Help me, my Father; protect my soul as I endure this persecution. Help me to stand as You would have me stand, speak what You would have me speak, and love with Your love even those who persecute me. Grant that I may provide protection for my family and an example of joy in suffering, that they may long to follow wherever You lead. In the name of the Father and the Son and the Holy Spirit. Amen.

"Do not think that I came to bring peace on earth. I
did not come to bring peace but a sword. For I have
come to 'set a man against his father, a daughter
against her mother, and a daughter-in-law against her
mother-in-law'; and 'a man's enemies will be those of
his own household.' He who loves father or mother
more than Me is not worthy of Me. And he who loves
son or daughter more than Me is not worthy of Me.
And he who does not take his cross and follow after
Me is not worthy of Me. He who finds his life will lose
it, and he who loses his life for My sake will find it."
(Matt. 10:34—39)

PRIDE

> *Pride, in any form is an enemy of man. Pride deceives*
> *us and insists we have no faults, are better than others*
> *and that we should hold ourselves above our fellow*
> *man. Pride makes us think that all our talents, all our*
> *blessings emanate from ourselves and our own efforts*
> *and abilities. Pride discounts God and inflates the*
> *individual. (Rev. Robert E. Lucas)*

O my God and my King, have mercy on me, pardon my prideful heart, and make me worthy to be Your simple servant. Open my eyes that I may see your truths and my deceptions in my lowly state. Let me forget myself and look only to You, the Lord and Master of my life. Grant me, O Lord, Your love, joy, peace, long-suffering, kindness, goodness, gentleness, self-control, humility, wisdom, and the courage to walk in Your ways. Amen.

> *Pride, more than anything else, deprives people of both*
> *their good deeds and the help of God. Where there*
> *is no light, there is darkness, and where there is no*
> *humility, pride takes its place. (St. Macarius)*

Guard the heart of my child, O Lord. He/she is being tempted to glorify him/herself through his/her gifts and abilities rather than to praise You for the gifts You have given. Remind him/her that You are mighty and worthy of praise. Grant that he/she may desire to use his/her abilities to glorify You, ever praying to You. In the name of the Father and the Son and the Holy Spirit. Amen.

Our self-love interferes and opposes every good deed of
ours, spoils it and corrupts it, and it especially hinders
the offering of pure prayer to God. (St. Ambrose)

Dear Lord Jesus, help us to fight against pride in our home
with kindness and humility. Let us be like St. Paul, who had
every reason to boast yet humbled himself before the throne of
our King and our God. Let our good works be done in secret
that we may obtain our reward in heaven. Your Word says, "A
man's pride will bring him low, but the humble in spirit will
retain honor" (Prov. 29:23). Help us to serve You and to serve
others in Your name. Let us remember that we need not think
of ourselves, for You Yourself care for us. Amen.

SPECIAL NEEDS—BEHAVIORAL, DEVELOPMENTAL, EMOTIONAL

I am mother to a child who has a heavy burden to carry.
This child doesn't fully understand body language or facial
expressions. He doesn't understand his own emotions much
beyond "happy" and "sad," and even those emotions he gets
mixed up sometimes. Some days he seems to need to bounce
his body off everyone and everything to figure out where his
body is in space and time. Everyone and everything doesn't
always appreciate this method. His volume control button
is broken—or perhaps we haven't found it yet. If there is
any sugar in the house, he will do anything to get it. He will
wake up in the middle of the night and sneak and steal. The

results are evident hours later when he is unable to control his body. He is like an addict looking for his next fix. And he is not at all pleasant when on his "drug." He becomes more physically imposing and louder. But there is one thing . . .

Sometimes, when parents have children who excel at being over-the-top challenging, whatever the special need might be, we have to find that "one thing" we can cling to that brings us hope. With all the behavior we have to deal with throughout each day, my son can have a very giving heart when it comes to his money. Last night he found some change left over from his allowance. He saw the little Food for the Hungry box we get at the beginning of each Lent (and generally don't turn in until the following Lent!). He took his money and without hesitation put it all into the box. He has taken toys and money his brothers left out and tried to make them his own. He has shown up with things from school that obviously belonged to someone else just because he couldn't control the temptation to take them. But he has *never* tried to take money from that box. He is always excited when he can add something to it and loves to pick it up to see how heavy it is getting.

My child regularly brings me to tears because of his behavior, and sometimes when I just think of the long, long road ahead of both of us, but this time the tears were because of a sweet, selfless gesture. Sometimes it's that "one thing" that makes all the difference.

> *Behold, children are a heritage from the* LORD.
> *(Ps. 127:3)*

Have mercy on me, O Lord, and calm my fatigued heart and mind. I feel out of control and overwhelmed by my child and what is required to care for his/her behavioral, developmental, or emotional needs. Help me so that in my distress I do not sin against You. Help me to take advantage of quiet moments, no matter how small, to seek Your holy counsel. Let me not forget to pray. Thank You that Your love for this child never changes or diminishes. Thank You that I can trust You for the strength I will need to parent this child today and that You provide hope for tomorrow. For You are holy, now and ever and unto ages of ages. Amen.

> *For You formed my inward parts;*
> *You covered me in my mother's womb.*
> *I will praise You, for I am fearfully and wonderfully*
>   *made;*
> *Marvelous are Your works,*
> *And that my soul knows very well.*
>   *(Ps. 139:13–14)*

My child seems out of control and I don't know what to do or how to pray. You formed this child and know what is going on physically, emotionally, and spiritually. If there is anything I have done, or neglected to do, show me the error of my ways that I may repent and follow Your plan. If the fault for the behavior is not mine, show me how to pray for my child, how to seek help for my child, and how to instruct my child in a way he/she will understand. Let my words be always kind, and may Your peace rest in my soul. When behavior is overwhelming, remind me at that very moment to seek Your will for the situation so that I may not fall into anger or frustration and lose ground. Let me remember that I am contending for the heart of my child and for the salvation of his/her soul. Help me to see this child as a blessing and this trial as lasting but for a moment in the light of eternity. Amen.

> *Then little children were brought to Him that He might put His hands on them and pray, but the disciples rebuked them. But Jesus said, "Let the little children come to Me, and do not forbid them; for of such is the kingdom of heaven." (Matt. 19:13–14)*

Prayers for the Family of a Baby with Special Needs ॐ

In the Name of the Father and the Son and the Holy Spirit. Amen. Lord Jesus Christ, who hold the universe in the palm of Your hand, bless and keep us Your servants and our infant/child (*Name*). You chose the fabric of his/her precious body and planned his/her every breath. Let us remember Your goodness and rejoice in Your holiness. Let us embrace the gift You have given as Your first choice from the riches of Your boundless treasure trove. May we see Your likeness which You have woven into our child's being. Let us hear the call You have for us and our child and respond with light hearts and open arms. Let surrender be our refuge and Your peace our nourishment. When we feed this child, remind us how You also touch our palates so we can taste Your goodness. When we change this child, remind us of the joyous changes You are bringing our hearts through. When we cuddle and rock our dear one, remind us of how dear this child is to You. May we take hold of

Your hands for guidance as this little one will grasp ours. When we sing to him/her, remind us that You too rejoice over us with singing. Amen.

Prayer for Children Who Have Difficulty Learning ↔

> Take heed that you do not despise one of these little ones, for I say to you that in heaven their angels always see the face of My Father who is in heaven. (Matt. 18:10)

Dear Lord, You who made the eyes of the blind to see and the deaf to hear, open the understanding of my child who is struggling to learn. Help him/her not to be discouraged. Show me how to best instruct my child and grant insight to any person participating in the education of my child. Above all, help my child to grasp the great love You have for him/her. Amen.

— 4 —

Prayers for the Sick, Dying & Dead

"I do so want God's will. Nothing more, nothing less, nothing else." (Kh. Terry Beck)

M Y FRIEND WAS DYING. My strong, godly, amazing godmother and friend. When I lived in California, she was my walking buddy. Up at 5:30 AM, she was my faithful companion, even when I wasn't faithful. We had some great conversations on those walks. We talked about memories, challenges, victories. We shared recipes, parenting tips, writing suggestions.

Those walks stopped in 2008 when my family moved to Colorado. *Those* walks stopped, but my friend and I did not stop walking. We continued to pray for each other as we faced life's challenges. I'd hear of victories, feel encouraged by her parenting tips and writing suggestions. When she told me they saw a spot on her pancreas, I had a sinking feeling. I just knew it was going to be bad. And it was.

When she turned fifty, she had a celebration of life as she embarked on the journey of being an "older woman." Each person present told a story or shared her impact on their life. Each of us had a rose which was attached to a wire, and the wire was fashioned into a wreath placed on her head like a crown.

Then, all of a sudden, there she was, caught in life's greatest transition. The body was pleading to live, and the will and mind were learning to surrender to her God and Savior. She has run the race, she has followed the path and carried her daily cross to the finish line.

The Bible tells us to run with perseverance the race set before us. During her life, I said we were running buddies in this race of life for the salvation of our souls. In this case, due to pain and fatigue, we became walking buddies. When the walking got too difficult, I crawled with her, and when she could no longer move, the prayers of all who loved her pushed her inch by inch toward the finish line.

Prayers for the sick, dying, and dead are very important in the lives of the Orthodox faithful. When everything seems hopeless, we still have the most powerful tool available to us:

prayer. We have the ability to cry out to a God who hears, and we have the saints who are no longer burdened with the limitations of this world who join us in prayer.

He Restores My Soul— Prayers for the Sick

Jesus Christ, my Lord and Savior, You became man and died on the cross for our salvation. You healed people of sickness and affliction through Your love and compassion. Visit me, Lord, and grant me strength to bear this sickness with which I am afflicted with patience, submission to Your will, and trust in Your loving care. I pray that You will bless the means used for my recovery and those who administer them. Grant that my sickness may be to my spiritual benefit and that I may live the rest of my life more faithfully according to Your will. For You are the source of life and healing, and to You I give praise and glory, now and forever. Amen.

Heavenly Father, physician of our souls and bodies, who have sent Your only-begotten Son and our Lord Jesus Christ to heal every sickness and infirmity, visit and heal also Your servant (*Name*) from all physical and spiritual ailments through the grace of Your Christ. Grant him/her patience in this sickness, strength of body and spirit, and recovery of health. Lord, You have taught us through Your word to pray for each other that we may be healed. I pray, heal Your servant (*Name*) and grant to him/her the gift of complete health. For You are the source of healing, and to You I give glory, Father, Son, and Holy Spirit. Amen.[5]

Prayer for a Sick Child ❧

O Lord Jesus Christ, who came into the world as a little child, and who, although being God, were subject to Your earthly parents: Grant Your child (*Name*) to bear cheerfully that which You are pleased to lay upon him/her and readily to obey those set over him/her by You. We beseech You, look mercifully upon him/her, and in Your great love grant him/her relief from his/her pain. O Lord, Son of God, send Your holy angel from heaven to guard, cherish, protect, visit, and defend Your child (*Name*), who is sick in his/her tender age. Stretch forth Your holy right hand upon him/her that, restored to the vigor of health, he/she may reach the fullness of years and serve You faithfully and gratefully all his/her life, and become an heir of Your Kingdom. For You are the Physician of our souls and bodies, O Christ our God, and to You we ascribe glory: to the Father, and to the Son, and to the Holy Spirit, now and ever and unto ages of ages. Amen.[6]

Thanksgiving after Recovery ❧

Almighty God and heavenly Father, You are the fountain of life and healing. I bless Your Holy Name and offer to You thanks for having delivered me from sickness and restored me to health. Grant me Your eternal grace, I pray, that I may live a new life in true obedience to You. Guide me to do Your will in all things, devoting my life to Your service. Thus living for You, may I be found worthy of Your kingdom, where You dwell in glory with Your Son and Your Holy Spirit forever. Amen.[7]

THE VALLEY OF THE SHADOW—
PRAYERS FOR THE DYING

Prayer for the Terminally Ill ॐ

Lord, Jesus Christ, who suffered and died for our sins that we may live, if during our life we have sinned in word, deed, or thought, forgive us in Your goodness and love. All our hope we put in You; protect your servant *(Name)* from all evil. We submit to Your will, and into Your hands we commend our souls and bodies. For a Christian end to our lives, peaceful, without shame and suffering, and for a good account before the awesome judgment seat of Christ, we pray to You, O Lord. Bless us, be merciful to us, and grant us life eternal. Amen.[8]

Prayers of Comfort for the Children of a Dying Parent ॐ

Our Father in heaven, bring comfort to the children of Your servant *(Name)* who is suffering from an incurable illness. I know You are able, with a word, to heal Your servant, but if You choose to bring him/her unto Yourself, help these children to know You are ever present and grieve along with them. Let them be aware of Your mercy and power, and remind them that You have overcome death and the grave. Reassure them during this trial that You are strong enough to provide for them during this dark hour, and that Your love for them and for Your servant *(Name)* endures forever. For You provide blessings for the poor in spirit, and to You we ascribe glory: to the Father and the Son and the Holy Spirit. Amen.

Prayers for a Peaceful End ↝

O Lord, even through the pain and discomfort Your servant has endured during this illness, allow him/her to depart in peace according to Your word. Let his/her eyes see glimpses of Your salvation and prepare him/her for this great separation of body and soul, that this trial may bring light and revelation to Your people. May *(Name)* know Your peace now and forever. Amen.

> *We are hard-pressed on every side, yet not crushed; we are perplexed, but not in despair; persecuted, but not forsaken; struck down, but not destroyed—always carrying about in the body the dying of the Lord Jesus, that the life of Jesus also may be manifested in our body. (2 Cor. 4:8–10)*

By Your work on the blessed Cross You conquered death. Grant strength to Your servant *(Name)* to conquer this world, pick up his/her cross, and follow You. As his/her body fails, remind him/her that Your love never fails. As his/her strength diminishes, remind him/her even in his/her last hour that he/she goes forth in Your strength. Help him/her to wrestle against the enemy to the very last that he/she may see Your salvation. In the name of the Father and the Son and the Holy Spirit. Amen.

O my Father, comfort my child *(Name)* as he/she prepares to enter into Your rest. Banish all fear and demonic influence. Send Your angels to provide comfort, and grant Your peace to this precious child as he/she struggles in his/her last battle on this earth. Help me in each moment to trust in Your goodness even though I feel undone. Let me be fully available to my child, physically and emotionally, as I was when You first blessed me to receive this child into my heart and home in Your name. For You are holy, now and ever and unto ages of ages. Amen.

THE HOUSE OF THE LORD—
PRAYERS FOR THE DEAD

> *The dead shall arise. Those in the tombs shall awake.*
> *All those on earth shall greatly rejoice. (Canon of*
> *Holy Saturday, Ode 5)*

Prayer for a Dead Child ᴗ

O Lord, who watch over children in the present life and in the world to come because of their simplicity and innocence of mind, abundantly satisfying them with a place in Abraham's bosom, bringing them to live in radiantly shining places where the spirits of the righteous dwell: receive in peace the soul of Your little servant *(Name)*, for You Yourself have said, "Let the little children come to Me, for of such is the kingdom of Heaven." Amen.[9]

O Holy Theotokos, Mother of our God, have mercy on me. You watched your Son in agony as He endured His passion; pray also for me, that I may bear this pain as my child crosses over into eternity. As I have received this child from your Son's gracious hands, I release him/her back into His heavenly care, where pain and suffering are no more. For He is a good God, and to Him we ascribe glory: to the Father, and to the Son, and to the Holy Spirit. Amen.

For our light affliction, which is but for a moment, is working for us a far more exceeding and eternal weight of glory, while we do not look at the things which are seen, but at the things which are not seen. For the things which are seen are temporary, but the things which are not seen are eternal. (2 Cor. 4:17–18)

Christ our eternal King and God, You have destroyed death and the devil by Your Cross and have restored man to life by Your Resurrection; give rest, Lord, to the soul of Your servant (*Name*) who has fallen asleep, in Your Kingdom, where there is no pain, sorrow, or suffering. In Your goodness and love for all men, pardon all the sins he/she has committed in thought, word, or deed, for there is no man or woman who lives and sins not; You only are without sin. For You are the Resurrection, the Life, and repose of Your servant (*Name*), departed this life, O Christ our God; and to You do we send up glory with Your Eternal Father and Your All-holy, Good, and Life-creating Spirit; both now and forever and to the ages of ages. Amen.[10]

Into Your hands, O Lord, I commend the soul of Your servant (*Name*), and beseech You to grant him/her rest in the place of Your rest, where all Your blessed saints repose, and where the light of Your countenance shines forever. And I beseech You also to grant that our present lives may be godly, sober, and blameless, that we too may be made worthy to enter into Your heavenly Kingdom with those we love but see no more: for You are the Resurrection, and the Life, and the repose of Your departed servant, O Christ our God, and unto You we ascribe glory: to the Father, and to the Son, and to the Holy Spirit, now and ever and unto ages of ages. Amen.[11]

Trisagion Memorial Prayer for the Departed ✌

O God of spirits and of all flesh, who have trampled down death and overthrown the devil, and given life to Your world, give, we beseech You, eternal rest to the soul of Your departed servant in a place of brightness, a place of verdure, a place of repose, from whence all pain, sorrow, and sighing have fled away.

Pardon, we beseech You, every transgression which may have been committed, whether by word or deed or thought. For there is no man who lives and does not commit a sin. You only are without sin, Your righteousness is everlasting, and Your word is the Truth.

For You are the Resurrection, and the Life, and the repose of Your departed servant, O Christ our God, and unto You we ascribe glory, together with the eternal Father and Your Most Holy, Good, and Life-giving Spirit, now and forever and for ages to come. Amen.

May our gracious and merciful Lord, who rose from the dead, Christ, our True God, through the intercessions of His Holy Mother and of all the saints, establish the soul of His departed servant in the mansions of the righteous; give him/her rest in the bosom of Abraham, and number his/her soul among the just, and have mercy upon us and save us.

Memory eternal!

Prayer after a Miscarriage ✌

O Sovereign Master, Lord our God, who were born of the all-pure Theotokos and Ever-Virgin Mary, and as an infant were laid in a manger: according to Your great mercy, have regard for this Your servant *(Name)* who has miscarried that which was conceived in her. Heal her suffering, granting to her, O loving Lord, health and strength of body and soul. Guard her with a shining angel from every assault of sickness and weakness and all inward torment. You who accept the innocence of infancy in Your Kingdom, comfort the mind of Your servant and bring her peace. Amen.[12]

Prayer for Unborn Infants ॐ

Remember, O Lord, Lover of Mankind, the souls of Your departed servants, infants who died accidentally in the wombs of Orthodox mothers from unknown cause, either from difficult birth or from some carelessness, and who therefore did not receive the Mystery of Holy Baptism. Baptize them, O Lord, in the sea of Your compassions, and save them by Your inexpressible grace. Amen.

O Lord of hosts, bring comfort to Your handmaid *(Name)* during this time of great loss. Hold her in Your loving hands and teach her to stand on the promise of the life of the world to come. Through the intercession of the Theotokos, O Savior, save us. Amen.

— 5 —

Confession
& the Beatitudes

HAVE YOU EVER GONE DAYS WITHOUT BATHING? You know, those days when the idea of a shower or a nice hot bath is just a fleeting thought. Try as you might, there is just no way to stuff it in between everything else that needs to be accomplished. And when you finally get that moment, perhaps a day or two (or more!) later, it feels like not only the sweat, dirt, and grime are being washed away, but layers of stress as well.

That's how it is with confession, but it is an internal cleansing that is beneficial for our salvation. Just as an external bath positively affects the aroma of our bodies, the spiritual cleansing of confession positively affects the aroma of our homes, and of course, our souls.

*When approaching the Mystery of Confession, one
must present himself with fear, humility and hope.
With fear as before God, who is angry with the sinner.
With humility—through recognition of one's sinfulness. With hope—for we approach the Child-loving
Father, who has sent His Son for our redemption,
who has taken our sins, nailed them to the Cross,
and washed them away with His most pure blood.*
(St. Macarius)

The Beatitudes are a useful tool when preparing for confession. We hear the beautiful words during each liturgy. Let us use them here as a way to honestly prepare our hearts so we too may reap the blessings of this sacrament.

*Enter into the Church and wash away your sins. For
there is a hospital for sinners and not a court of law.*
(St. John Chrysostom)

THE BEATITUDES

✤ *Blessed are the poor in spirit, for theirs is the kingdom of
heaven.*
Have I truly recognized my complete dependence
on God? Have I been proud, arrogant, and self-
righteous in my ways? Have I been selfish, possessive,
and self-seeking? Have I sought after status, power,
and wealth?

✠   *Blessed are those who mourn, for they shall be comforted.*
Have I endured difficulties and afflictions with faith
and patience? Have I felt sadness for the sufferings of
the poor, the hungry, and addicted; the sick, the lonely,
and the sinful of the world? Have I truly been sorrow-
ful for my sins and faults?

✠   *Blessed are the meek, for they shall inherit the earth.*
Have I tried to serve or rather to dominate others at
home, school, work, office, church, and elsewhere?
Have I nursed ill will against anyone? Have I been
resentful, bitter, unforgiving, or insulting and abusive
to others? Have I loved my enemies?

✠   *Blessed are those who hunger and thirst for righteousness, for
they shall be satisfied.*
Have I truly yearned for God's will to be done in all
things? Have I worked for justice in my family, society,
and the world in ways within my reach? Have I tried
to cultivate a righteous life through prayer, fasting,
worship, receiving Holy Communion, and deeds of
love toward others?

✠   *Blessed are the merciful, for they shall obtain mercy.*
Have I shown compassion and help toward the poor,
hungry, lonely, and needy around me? Have I tried to

understand and forgive others? Have I been indifferent, judgmental, or legalistic?

✠ *Blessed are the pure in heart, for they shall see God.*
Have I loved goodness, purity, and holiness? Have
I succumbed to evil motives and intentions? Have
I given way to impure thoughts, words, or deeds?
Have I been guilty of bias and prejudice? Have I been
hypocritical, pretentious, or self-indulgent to sinful
passions?

✠ *Blessed are the peacemakers, for they shall be called sons of God.*
Do I have God's peace in my heart? Have I been
unfairly angry, aggressive, or impatient? Have I worked
for peace at home, work, church, and in society? Have I
been irritable, polemical, or divisive?

✠ *Blessed are those who are persecuted for righteousness' sake, for
theirs is the kingdom of heaven.*
Have I complained when persecuted for God's sake?
Have I prayed for my persecutors? Have I failed to
defend anyone in the truth for fear of humiliation or
persecution? Have I had the courage to stand up for
what is right despite criticism, ridicule, or persecution?

✠ *Blessed are you when they revile you and persecute you on my
account; rejoice and be glad, for your reward is great in heaven.*
Is the joy of Christ in my heart even in trying

moments? Have I been pessimistic, despondent, or despairing? Have I truly delighted in the promise of God's treasures in heaven?[13]

Prayer before Confession

O God and Lord of all, who have power over every breath and soul, the only One able to heal me, hear the prayer of me, the wretched one, and, having put him to death, destroy the serpent nestling within me by the descent of the All-Holy and Life-Creating Spirit. And grant me, poor and naked of all virtue, to fall with tears at the feet of my spiritual father, and call his holy soul to have mercy on me. And grant, O Lord, to my heart humility and good thoughts, suitable to a sinner who has consented to repent to You, and do not abandon to the end the one soul that has united itself to You and has confessed You, and instead of all the world has chosen You and preferred You. For You know, O Lord, that I want to save myself, and that my evil habit is an obstacle. But all things are possible to You, O Master, which are impossible for man. Amen. (St. Symeon the New Theologian)

Confession with Children

How often should I, or my children, participate in confession?

The question of how often you should make confession is best left to the counsel of your spiritual father or mother.

They know your family and are asking God for insight concerning your specific life situations. Encouraging your children to seek the counsel of a spiritual father or mother will help get them into the practice of seeking out godly counsel in this world, which provides so many false prophets to counsel our youth. Don't be afraid to ask your priest for guidance—that's what they are there for.

How can I encourage my children to prepare for confession?

When my children were small, I would give them a child-friendly version of the Ten Commandments to review and a piece of paper so they could write down their confessions. I saw the confessions of my very little ones because I helped them write them down, but I never looked at the confessions of my older children because I wanted them to be able to give a full confession without fear of what mom might see. This was successful for a number of years until they could start seeking out confession on their own. And it is important to lead by example. If we humble ourselves and participate in confession, our children are much more likely to participate willingly as well.

Sometimes I have seen my children burdened by something they initially don't want to share with me. It takes all my self-control not to require them to confide in me, because deep down I want be the one who encourages them and whom they can trust with anything. But those moments provide the perfect opportunity to encourage them to start seeking out the counsel of the priest and to view the Church as the spiritual hospital we often talk about. We want them to find healing, not from us, but from the Lord. This is part of helping them work out their own salvation with fear and trembling.

Prayers after Confession

O almighty and merciful God, I truly thank You for the forgiveness of my sins; bless me, O Lord, and help me always, that I may ever do that which is pleasing to You, and sin no more. Amen.

O Lord God of my salvation, the Savior and Benefactor of my soul, I am truly sorry for my every transgression, and I firmly resolve never again to offend You by my sins, and sincerely promise to amend my way of life. Implant in me the fear of Your blessed commandments, that I may trample down all carnal appetites and may lead a godly life, both thinking and doing such things as are well-pleasing to You. I pray You, grant me the grace of Your Holy Spirit, that thus strengthened, I may shun all evil deeds, works, words, and thoughts, and may avoid all the snares of the evil one. Shine in my heart with the true sun of Your righteousness, enlighten my mind, and guard all my senses, that walking uprightly in the way of Your statutes, I may attain to life eternal. Amen.

O sovereign Master, who love mankind, lead me in Your way that I may walk in Your truth. Make glad my heart that I may fear Your holy name. O Lord, mighty in mercy and gracious in strength, aid, comfort, and save me as I put my trust in Your holy name. Rebuke me not, O Lord, in Your displeasure, neither punish me in Your wrath, but show me Your great mercy and compassion, O physician and healer of my soul. O merciful Savior, blot out all my transgressions, for I am heartily sorry for having offended You. Grant me Your grace that I may avoid my previous evil ways. Strengthen me, O mighty one, to withstand those temptations before which I am weak, that I may avoid all future sin. Keep me under Your protection and in the shadow of Your wings, that I may serve You, praise You, and glorify You all the days of my life. Amen.

A WORD ON SPIRITUAL FATHERS

> *A spiritual father, like a signpost, merely indicates the way, but you yourself must follow the path. If the spiritual father points the way, but his disciple does not move, and will not go anywhere, then he will simply rot at that signpost. (St. Nikon)*

Okay, I'll admit it. Sometimes I don't want to go to confession. Sometimes I don't want to take inventory of my actions, words, and thoughts and tell someone else those private, despicable details. Sometimes I don't want to seek holy counsel; instead I desire to wallow, or ignore, or justify. Other times I think, "Hey, I've done pretty well"—that is, until I look over the Ten Commandments or the Beatitudes.

What is a mama to do? What do we do when we wear so many hats and drop that blasted ball so often? As Christians we are told we are to take up our crosses and follow Christ, but sometimes, whether out of pride, fear, or zeal, we pick up a cross not meant for us. Seeking the counsel of our priest as we participate in confession can help us lay down those things not meant for us to carry so we can, through the strength of Christ, embrace our own cross.

We try to be positive examples to our children. We try to balance it all. Sometimes we feel like we're a mood swing away from crazy. Thanks be to God that He made women and, while not a woman, He completely understands us, hormonal shifts and all. When lamenting over Jerusalem, He compares Himself to a mother hen wanting to gather her chicks under her wings (Matt. 23:37). He comforts us the same way a mother comforts her child (Is. 66:13). We can trust His loving heart toward us as mothers, for He also has a special place in His heart for His own mother, the Theotokos.

When we fall down in our Christian walk, seeking out a spiritual mother or father helps us as we prepare for confession and as we attempt to walk in spiritual safety through this life. Saint Leo of Optina says, "If a person sincerely seeks salvation with his whole heart, God will lead him to a true instructor. Do not worry, each will find the one who is just right for him."

We are encouraged against going from spiritual father to spiritual father, because we are not shopping for the answer that sounds best to us in response to life's problems. Rather, we seek the counsel of one spiritual advisor so that we can, through his or her humble direction, continue to progress further in our Christian walk.

— 6 —

Prayers of Blessing
& Thanksgiving

*That which is done with a blessing is greatly pleasing
to God; so let us live that every small step of ours is
blessed. (St. Anthony)*

IT STARTED WITH A FIGHT. Loud voices can be heard so
clearly when one is trying to sleep. Of course I wasn't
sleeping at that point, but I was daydreaming about real
dreaming. The oldest boy and youngest boy each got up on
the wrong side of the planet this morning. Each one blamed
the other, was offended by the notion that he should take
responsibility for his own part in the fight, and was willing to
lose privilege after privilege before this first fight was finally
resolved. "Maybe it's not so bad," I thought, "we just got it

out of the way early today." Ha! Of course not, that would be too easy.

The second fight was after breakfast and over Legos. There was a miscommunication, and words too big for the situation were used to express frustration. I reprimanded the younger, who had destroyed the creation of the elder. I discussed with the older child the need to remove himself from heated situations and encouraged him to use more appropriate words to express his frustration. You would have thought I was an alien with four heads. I made sure each head said the same thing, and we concluded our interview.

Just before we left for a counseling appointment, the doorbell rang. Of course, today had to be the day our wonderful social worker came for her annual surprise visit. Apparently, moments before she entered my home, our lovely, severely undertrained dog brought in a gift of feathers from our recently departed chickens (victims of foxes, we think) and deposited them on the floor in the living room. It's always awkward when you have a guest, and a normally somewhat clean room is suddenly cluttered, and you feel the need to explain yourself but end up looking more foolish than if you'd just kept your mouth shut.

Fortunately, our social worker truly is a lovely woman and already loved our family. She knew we were in a hurry, and as I escorted her to her car, by way of the garage so the undertrained dogs couldn't maul her, two mud-covered creatures burst through the outside garage door, laughing and shaking their rear ends. The youngest (six at the time) had neglected to put on underwear this particular morning and so became an exhibitionist when his mud-laden sweats fell down around his ankles during one of his dance turns.

The social worker left, and I ran out the door to a van that took five tries to start. We finally made it to counseling for the oldest boy when I received a text from my eldest daughter that read, "Brother #3 is naked and I can't turn on the hose." *Sigh.* I finally communicated through texts, while trying to show my focused support and encouragement to my oldest son, who of course refused to tell the counselor anything because he was still throwing a silent tantrum over his loss of video game privileges.

I usually stand there puzzled, or crying, on days like this. I search my mind for how my girls behaved when they were little, and I am comforted. Not because they were little angels (although none of them ever yelled "I hate you" at me or one another), but because I do remember the day they found the tempera paint and painted the toilet, washer and dryer, their bunk bed, the carpet, and the walls. I remember them sneaking into the kitchen and stealing the freshly made bread. They didn't steal the whole loaf—no, that would be too boring—they hollowed it out by carefully taking handfuls from the center, and I'd be none the wiser until

I went to cut some in the morning. They snuck sugar cubes and candy. They used to strip and run outside. The oldest threw mud clots at an old woman's car as she drove by—I certainly got an earful for that one.

With all the mud, language, and crazy antics of my children, I still find myself feeling so blessed and would love to be blessed with more. When I asked my second daughter how many children she thought we should have, she said "sixteen." I suggested we might as well have twenty, to which she replied "Twenty?! That would be too many." Ha! Children truly are blessings even with the arguments, muddy footprints all over the floor, peeing in the—uh—wrong places, adolescent hormonal explosions, or artistic mood swings. I am blessed by it all!

How often do we miss out on giving a blessing to our children or thanking the Lord for His love and mercy in every situation? The Holy Scriptures say:

> *Rejoice in the Lord always. Again I will say, rejoice!*
> *Let your gentleness be known to all men. The Lord is*
> *at hand. Be anxious for nothing, but in everything by*
> *prayer and supplication, with thanksgiving, let your*
> *requests be known to God; and the peace of God, which*
> *surpasses all understanding, will guard your hearts and*
> *minds through Christ Jesus. (Phil. 4:4   7)*

This doesn't mean we proclaim, "I'm so glad I lost my job!" or "This cancer thing is great!" but it does mean that even in the midst of life's greatest struggles, we can rejoice because Christ has come. He has defeated sin and death and called us to be His sons and daughters. Let us therefore rejoice! Let us pray to the Lord with thanksgiving. Let us pray blessings upon our children, for the God we serve is good, and His love endures forever.

Before School

O Lord our God, who love my children so faithfully, bless each step my children take this day. May their minds be full of Your truth, and may their mouths boldly speak Your praise. Enable them to stand as a light on their campuses. Keep them from the temptation of peer pressure or any influence that would lead them in a direction contrary to Your will. Allow them to live godly lives balanced with grace and compassion, both in front of their peers and in private. Help them to avoid fruitless arguments or any kind of dispute. Direct them in all their dealings with peers and teachers. Let them be honest, trustworthy, and hard-working. Keep them from any word or deed that would reflect negatively on You, O Lord. In the Name of the Father and of the Son and of the Holy Spirit. Amen.

> *You think that it would be better for your son to be with you all the time, but who knows? With you, if God permits, he could become spoiled, while in the hands of others, preserved from harm. In the end, regardless of where your children might be, with you or in the care of someone else, instill in them Christian principles and*

> *entrust them to God and the intercession of the Mother*
> *of God. (St. Macarius)*

O Christ our Savior, as I endeavor to homeschool my children this day, grant me the ability to see the needs of each child. Let me be faithful in preparing their daily work and joyful in my instruction. Help my children's hearts and minds to be open to spiritual lessons and grant them understanding during their studies. Let me take every opportunity to teach my children of Your goodness in such a way that they will desire a deeper knowledge of and closer relationship with their Lord. Help us to treat one another with mutual respect and kindness, and let all instruction and correction be done in love. When the official time for lessons is over, let me continue to teach my children Your ways, for You are a good and loving God. In Your mercy, teach my children Your statutes, help them to understand Your commandments, and enlighten them with Your precepts. For You are holy, now and ever and unto ages of ages. Amen.

> *Your word is a lamp to my feet*
> *And a light to my path. (Ps. 119:105)*

Bless my children, O Lord, with all that is necessary for them to be successful in their studies. Grant my children motivation, that they may do their work faithfully as unto the Lord. Grant my children the ability to comprehend their instruction; bring light to their understanding, O Lord. Grant my children discernment, that they may not forsake Your teachings. For You are a good God and You love all mankind. Amen.

CHASTITY

> *Every man who loves purity and chastity becomes the*
> *temple of God. (St. Ephrem the Syrian)*

Dear Lord Jesus, thank You for the gift of chastity which You have given my children. Help them to desire to keep themselves pure in heart, mind, and body. Protect their innocence, strengthen their sense of morality, and grant them discernment. Help them to practice restraint when tempted by sin that cunningly presents itself as something beautiful or good. And if my children have fallen into temptation, bring them to repentance and back into communion with You, accepting Your love, forgiveness, and cleansing. For You are a good God, and to You we ascribe glory, to the Father and the Son and the Holy Spirit. Amen.

> *Offer to the Lord the weakness of your nature, fully*
> *acknowledging your own powerlessness, and imper-*
> *ceptibly you will receive the gift of chastity. (St. John*
> *Climacus)*

O Lord, help me as a mother to be pure of heart and mind. Let me refuse to participate in coarse joking, obscene words, or conversations that do not honor You. When questionable situations arise, let me set an example for my children, keeping false humility and judgment far from me. For You are holy, now and ever and unto ages of ages. Amen.

CHURCH

*The church is for us an earthly heaven where God
Himself abides and looks upon those standing there.
Therefore we must stand orderly in church, with great
reverence. Let us love the church and let us be zealous
towards it. It is a comfort and consolation for us in
time of sorrows and of joys. (St. Hilarion)*

Just when I was beginning to wonder if my boys were even listening during church, the Lord brought us a dead bird.

It was an overcast Sunday. After rest time, my boys went outside to play. I was expecting the usual American Ninja Warrior training attempts with the obstacles they had created. Or maybe they'd tire themselves on the trampoline by trying to bounce one another over the net (attempted, never achieved). Suddenly my youngest burst through the door, telling me to come quickly. "There's a black squishy thing out there you've got to see! It's an emergency!"

I braced myself for what I might see. Some half-dead snake perhaps (at which point I wouldn't be able to help them if they were scared—it's hard to help while screaming and standing on top of the kitchen island). Thankfully it was only a dead bird. The older two boys asked if they could get the medical gloves we use for picking up dog poop and take a closer look at the bird. I had no problem with that as long as *I* didn't have to touch it.

I walked away, but a few minutes later I went to check

on them to make sure they weren't being disrespectful to the bird. I'm fine with scientific study, which may include opening the chest cavity to see what everything looks like, but I do have a problem with breaking bones or popping off a head just to see what it might feel like to destroy a creature—even a dead creature. To my delight, not only were they being respectful, they were planning a burial for the poor thing.

My youngest was the gravedigger while my older two were clergy. My middle guy got his blue belt from his martial arts class and wrapped it, as best he could, like an Orthodox deacon's stole over his white T-shirt. The oldest came out in what looked a Little Red Riding Hood cape, with his yellow martial arts belt representing his stole.

They placed the bird in a clear empty tennis-ball container and began the service by singing their rendition of a burial song: "O give thanks unto the Lord for He is good, alleluia. For His mercy endureth forever, alleluia." Of course their version didn't include all the words, but it was a good attempt. The oldest held out our cross-shaped wind-whirl thing for the other boys to kiss and then sang as they circled the grave several times. He took hold of his martial arts belt, held it up over the grave, and blessed it with the sign of the cross while the young deacon picked dried weeds to represent the flowers they needed to place on the grave. The bird was laid in the grave, and they placed the weeds on top of the "casket" while the "deacon" faced the attendees (me) to announce the service that would be happening directly following the burial.

The gravedigger piled dirt atop the grave as the "priest" poured little vials of holy water over the grave and blessed it with a large rugged cross they had made by nailing two pieces of wood together. They bowed to the icon of the Holy Trinity and again circled the grave, singing.

Finally the "priest" gave a moving homily and said a prayer over the "righteous bird" that it might "live again in heaven and live for good this time." The gravedigger whispered something into the "deacon's" ear, calling him away into the clubhouse. Right when the "priest" finished, out came the two youngest and dramatically said, "I'm Conan—and I'm Thor—and we're here to pump (stomp) you up!" in their best Arnold Schwarzenegger accents (learned at camp).

Then they went back to arguing and fighting, but a moment of holiness had taken place. And a piece of me wonders if that bird did get to heaven with a surprised look on his face while a bewildered St. Peter ushered him into the Kingdom by the faith and devotion of these little ones.

O Lord of Sabaoth, bless my children, who are made in Your image, to be as living icons. Let us have ears to hear Your word, eyes to see Your glory, and a mouth that speaks Your truth in love and mercy. When we enter Your sanctuary and prepare ourselves to receive Your very body and blood, let us not become distracted by the cares of the world we bring in with us; but rather remind us to lay our cares at Your feet as we sing "Lord have mercy." Grant us the willingness to listen and the ability to hear. Keep us from disturbing those around us, and shield all Your people from every attack of the enemy sent to keep us from receiving the healing of soul and body through Blessed Communion. In the name of the Father and the Son and the Holy Spirit. Amen.

COURAGE

Genuine holy courage is always united with the feeling of deep humility. (St. Nikon)

Dear Lord, please grant my children courage. Grant them the courage to trust You, the courage to speak the truth in love, and the courage to walk in Your ways. Strengthen them in difficult situations and remind them that they are never alone, for You are with them even to the end of the age. Strengthen them in Your love that they may endeavor to do their best in all things, try new things, and always do the right thing. Amen.

> *Wait on the Lord;*
> *Be of good courage,*
> *And He shall strengthen your heart;*
> *Wait, I say, on the Lord!*
> *(Ps. 27:14)*

Diligence

*But also for this very reason, giving all diligence, add
to your faith virtue, to virtue knowledge, to knowledge
self-control, to self-control perseverance, to perseverance godliness, to godliness brotherly kindness, and to
brotherly kindness love. For if these things are yours and
abound, you will be neither barren nor unfruitful in the
knowledge of our Lord Jesus Christ. (2 Peter 1:5–8)*

Thank You, Lord Jesus Christ, for the bodies You have blessed
us with. Thank You for the ways You have provided for us to
use these bodies for Your glory. Thank You that regardless of
the limitations our bodies may have, You have given ways for
us to diligently serve You. There is always the temptation to be
lazy, to take the easy way or put things off. But You, O Lord, call
us to be diligent in all things. Grant my children the strength
of heart, mind, and body to follow through with their commit-
ments to the very best of their ability. Let them be faithful to
accept instruction and apply what they have learned. Let them
be attentive to their spiritual lives, persevering in such a way
that they may receive the prize. Let them be industrious, not
shying away from responsibility or difficulty. Most of all, let
their efforts be fruitful as they grow in the knowledge of our
Lord Jesus Christ. For You are holy, now and ever and unto
ages of ages. Amen.

*But, beloved, we are confident of better things
concerning you, yes, things that accompany salvation,
though we speak in this manner. For God is not unjust
to forget your work and labor of love which you have
shown toward His name, in that you have ministered
to the saints, and do minister. And we desire that each*

> *one of you show the same diligence to the full assurance*
> *of hope until the end, that you do not become sluggish,*
> *but imitate those who through faith and patience*
> *inherit the promises. (Heb. 6:9–12)*

O Father God, help me, Your servant, to be faithful in the tasks You place before me. Help me to be just as diligent in praising my children when their efforts are fruitful as I am in training and disciplining them. Show me daily how to run my race in the joyful service of others. Order my time and priorities that every moment of my day and purpose of my heart glorifies You. In the name of the Father and the Son and the Holy Spirit. Amen.

FAITH

> *I implore you to live piously in order that you might*
> *preserve your Orthodox faith, in order that no one and*
> *nothing, no circumstances and no kind of sorrow can*
> *turn you away from it. For this you absolutely must pray,*
> *seeking God's help to keep your faith pure. (St. Nikon)*

Dear Lord, strengthen the faith of my children that they will not only glorify Your Name with their lips but fully believe in You as their Lord and Savior. Let their faith grow that "no one and nothing, no circumstances and no kind of sorrow" can turn them away from the One Holy Catholic and Apostolic Church. Help them to embrace the faith as their own, that they may be willing to accept the blessings along with any persecutions they may encounter for Your Name's sake. For You are holy, and to You we ascribe glory, to the Father and the Son and the Holy Spirit. Amen.

*A woman cannot live without faith. Either she lives
for a period of time without faith and then soon
returns to faith in God, or she quickly begins to go to
pieces. It is another matter for a man: it is possible for
him to live without faith. He hardens completely and
becomes a pillar of salt, and so he lives, stiff and cold.
But a woman cannot live like this. (St. Barsanuphius)*

By faith Rahab was delivered from the destruction of Jericho
because she believed in the power of the God of the Israelites.
Help me, O Lord, to have that same faith, the faith to stand
firm even when the walls of life seem to be falling all around
me. Thank You that I can trust You with each member of my
family, knowing that Your love for them and hope for their salvation is greater than mine. Help me to remember that "I have
been crucified with Christ; it is no longer I who live, but Christ
lives in me; and the *life* which I now live in the flesh I live by
faith in the Son of God, who loved me and gave Himself for
me" (Gal. 2:20). For You are blessed, now and ever and unto
ages of ages. Amen.

FORGIVENESS

*Whoever prays for those who hurt him lays the
demons low; but he who opposes his affronter is bound
to the demons. (St. Mark the Ascetic)*

All Holy Trinity, help my children to open their hearts to forgive. Teach them to forgive others just as You have forgiven
them. Protect them from being easily offended and touch their
hearts that they may feel compassion and be compelled to pray

for those who have hurt them. For You are holy, now and ever and unto ages of ages. Amen.

> *The forgiveness of insults is a sign of true love, free*
> *from hypocrisy. For thus the Lord also loved this*
> *world. (St. Mark the Ascetic)*

Lord Jesus Christ, You who came into the world to save sinners, thank You for making Your forgiveness available to me; grant me the humility to forgive those who have hurt me. Let love replace hatred and kindness, bitterness. Let negative reminders be banished as I rejoice in the knowledge that You have forgiven me my sins. In the name of the Father and the Son and the Holy Spirit. Amen.

FRIENDSHIP

> *The righteous should choose his friends carefully,*
> *For the way of the wicked leads them astray. (Prov. 12:26)*

O Holy Father, grant my children wisdom as they develop friendships. Bless them with friends who desire to be friends of Christ above all, and make them faithful companions, encouraging one another, as they walk the narrow but glorious path that leads to You. Direct my children to seek out good company and, if none be available, grant them the strength and courage to stand alone. For You are holy and to You we ascribe all glory, honor, and power. In the Father and the Son and the Holy Spirit. Amen.

HAPPINESS

> *Beloved, do not think it strange concerning the fiery*
> *trial which is to try you, as though some strange thing*
> *happened to you; but rejoice to the extent that you*
> *partake of Christ's sufferings, that when His glory is*
> *revealed, you may also be glad with exceeding joy. If*
> *you are reproached for the name of Christ, blessed are*
> *you, for the Spirit of glory and of God rests upon you.*
> (1 Peter 4:12—14)

There is happiness for those who trust in You, O Lord our God, and joy as we participate in Your sufferings. Bless my children to be of good cheer, willing helpers and peacemakers, looking for Your likeness in each person they serve. Fill them with the happiness of heaven that they may share that joy with others in Your Name and for Your glory. For You are holy, now and ever and unto ages of ages. Amen.

> *Be glad in the Lord and rejoice, you righteous;*
> *And shout for joy, all you upright in heart!*
> (Ps. 32:11)

Thank You for allowing us to rejoice in Your goodness, O Lord of hosts, that we may proclaim Your mercy even in the midst of afflictions. Direct my children in righteousness and bless them with the joy of Your salvation. You who are able to keep their feet from stumbling and to present them faultless before the presence of Your glory with exceeding joy, we give glory to You as our God and Savior, who alone are wise and loving toward all mankind. To You we ascribe glory, honor, and power, in the name of the Father and the Son and the Holy Spirit. Amen.

> *Now godliness with contentment is great gain. For we*
> *brought nothing into this world, and it is certain we*
> *can carry nothing out. And having food and clothing,*
> *with these we shall be content. (1 Tim. 6:6—8)*

Grant to us all, O Heavenly King, peace of heart and true contentment with however You choose to provide for our needs. Let us appreciate the smallest blessing and rejoice even in the midst of trials because of Your great goodness. Help us to be joyful at all times and look forward with gladness to the world to come. For You are good and love mankind. Amen.

Humility

> *Therefore if there is any consolation in Christ, if*
> *any comfort of love, if any fellowship of the Spirit,*
> *if any affection and mercy, fulfill my joy by being*
> *like-minded, having the same love, being of one accord,*
> *of one mind. Let nothing be done through selfish ambi-*
> *tion or conceit, but in lowliness of mind let each esteem*
> *others better than himself. Let each of you look out not*
> *only for his own interests, but also for the interests of*
> *others. (Phil. 2:1—4)*

O Holy Trinity, protect my children from selfishness but instead grant them humility and love toward one another. Let them settle disputes quickly and without seeking to prove themselves right. Let them do good for others without the expectation of anything in return. As You, Lord, humbled Yourself to be but a servant here on earth, let my children embrace that same humility with gladness. Let love for You be their first rule, and love for their brother as themselves their guide in attitude and behavior. Let them accept lowly tasks with joy and thanksgiving, and let them not think themselves above kind service toward others. Amen.

> *Humility is the only thing that no devil can imitate.*
> *(St. John Climacus)*

Help me, O Lord, to keep as a constant reminder the publican who acknowledged his sinfulness and with all humility asked for Your mercy. Show me any self-serving attitudes in me that I may repent and follow Your ways. Help me to present a good example of unconditional love and humility to my children. For You are good and You love mankind. Amen.

> *They asked an elder, "What is humility?" The elder*
> *said, "When your brother sins against you, and you*
> *forgive him, before he repents before you."*

LIBERALITY

> *Do not become harsh and unmerciful. Think that*
> *behind him who seeks charity from you, is the Lord*
> *Himself. . . . Give charity for your own benefit and for*
> *the benefit of those who are really poor. The Lord will*
> *reward you. (St. John Chrysostom)*

Dear Lord, bless my children with a heart of giving, that they may search for Your likeness in each person they meet and serve them "as unto the Lord." Let them be courteous, compassionate, and willing to release every earthly treasure for the sake of the Kingdom of God. When they are challenged to withhold goodness from another, let them remember the

Cross and Your willingness to present Yourself as a sacrifice for the salvation of their souls. For You are blessed, now and ever and unto ages of ages. Amen.

> *And the King will answer and say to them, "Assuredly,*
> *I say to you, inasmuch as you did it to one of the least*
> *of these My brethren, you did it to Me." (Matt. 25:40)*

O Lord of hosts, help me to be charitable to all in word, action, and thought. Help me not grow weary in doing good but to be compassionate toward everyone I encounter, especially my children. Help me to remember that they too are working out their salvation. Let me encourage them with kindness and lead by example. For to You we ascribe glory, honor, and praise, to the Father and the Son and the Holy Spirit. Amen.

LOVE

> *Love suffers long and is kind; love does not envy; love*
> *does not parade itself, is not puffed up; does not behave*
> *rudely, does not seek its own, is not provoked, thinks*
> *no evil; does not rejoice in iniquity, but rejoices in the*
> *truth; bears all things, believes all things, hopes all*
> *things, endures all things. (1 Cor. 13:4–7)*

O Christ our God, bless my children with the kind of love that suffers long and is kind—a love that is strong enough to love the unlovely and wide enough to embrace all people for Your Name's sake. Let Your love guide them to rejoice in Your truth, bear the things You allow into their lives, believe completely in Your goodness, and endure all things. Help them to love those who hate them and have compassion on those who persecute them, that they may be found faithful on the day of judgment. In the name of the Father and the Son and the Holy Spirit, now and ever and unto ages of ages. Amen.

The Perfect Person's Rule of Life

The perfect person does not only try to avoid evil. Nor does he do good for fear of punishment, still less in order to qualify for the hope of a promised reward.

The perfect person does good through love.

His actions are not motivated by desire for personal benefit, so he does not have personal advantage as his aim. But as soon as he has realized the beauty of doing good, he does it with all his energies and in all that he does.

He is not interested in fame, or a good reputation, or a human or divine reward.

The rule of life for a perfect person is to be in the image and likeness of God.
(St. Clement of Alexandria)

PATIENCE

Do not be cast down over the struggle—the Lord loves a brave warrior. The Lord loves the soul that is valiant.
(St. Silouan the Athonite)

Thank You, O Lord, for the gift of patience, difficult though it may seem. Help me to recognize the trying situations I face as opportunities to practice patience. Help me to be a messenger of peace and calm on Your behalf. Let me fight diligently—not against any person, but against the enemy of our souls. Grant me Your courage as I submit myself to Your perfect will. Let my patient endurance be only a reflection of Your love and goodness in my life. Amen.

> *The mercy of God is hidden in sufferings not of our choice; and if we accept such sufferings patiently, they bring us to repentance and deliver us from everlasting punishment. (St. Kosmas Aitolos)*

Dear Lord, bless my children with patient endurance as they face the trials and persecutions in this world. Bless them with the understanding that the testing of their faith produces patience. Let them see the benefit of storing up treasures in heaven rather than seeking justice for themselves on earth. Help them to trust You to justify them and deliver them from unwarranted maltreatment. Even if You choose not to deliver them from their trial, help them to stand firm in the faith to the very last. For You are holy, and to You we ascribe glory, to the Father and to the Son and to the Holy Spirit, now and ever and unto ages of ages. Amen.

> *My brethren, count it all joy when you fall into various trials, knowing that the testing of your faith produces patience. (James 1:2–3)*

PEACE

> *That I am a monk and you are a layman is of no importance . . . rather that we are both in the light*

> *of the Holy Spirit. . . . Acquire peace, and thousands*
> *around you will be saved. (St. Seraphim of Sarov)*

O Lord Jesus Christ, You who are the Prince of Peace, grant peace to my children. In stressful situations, let them know Your peace. When they are faced with many challenges and the darkness and confusion of the world seem overwhelming, let them know that peace which surpasses all understanding. Guide, O Lord, their hearts and minds through the power of Your very self. Amen.

> *Be anxious for nothing, but in everything by prayer*
> *and supplication, with thanksgiving, let your requests*
> *be made known to God; and the peace of God, which*
> *surpasses all understanding, will guard your hearts and*
> *minds through Christ Jesus. (Phil. 4:6—7)*

PEACEFUL SLEEP

> *I will both lie down in peace, and sleep;*
> *For You alone, O Lord, make me dwell in safety.*
>   *(Ps. 4:8)*

Dear Lord Jesus, Prince of Peace, bless my children with peaceful and undisturbed sleep. Let them fill their minds with the holy things of God by day that they may dwell on Your goodness by night. Protect their minds from every evil thought, memory, or attack from the evil one. Bring to mind the words from the Liturgy that sing of Your glory and proclaim Your holy power and love. Remind them, O Lord, that You never sleep nor slumber and it is You who keep watch over them.

May they lie down in peace and sleep, reminded that You alone make them dwell in safety. For You are holy, now and ever and unto ages of ages. Amen.

> *When you lie down, you will not be afraid;*
> *Yes, you will lie down and your sleep will be sweet.*
> *Do not be afraid of sudden terror,*
> *Nor of trouble from the wicked when it comes;*
> *For the Lord will be your confidence,*
> *And will keep your foot from being caught.*
> *(Prov. 3:24–26)*

SAFETY

> *He who dwells in the secret place of the Most High*
> *Shall abide under the shadow of the Almighty.*
> *I will say of the LORD, "He is my refuge and my*
> *   fortress;*
> *My God, in Him I will trust." (Ps. 91:1–2)*

Thank You, O Lord, that we can trust in Your protection. Grant safety to my children as they face each day and each new situation. I beg for their physical safety, but even more, that You would allow what is necessary for the salvation of their souls. Protect them against the wiles of the enemy and teach them to seek Your protection and take refuge in You. For You are a good God and You love mankind. Amen.

> *The name of the Lord is a strong tower;*
> *The righteous run to it and are safe.*
> *(Prov. 18:10)*

SALVATION

> *Our salvation consists in faith and hope in the mercy*
> *of God, and the devotion of ourselves and all of us to*
> *His holy will. (St. Macarius)*

Thank You, Jesus, for the gift of salvation You offer to all mankind. Let my children see the benefit of working out their salvation with fear and trembling all the days of their lives. May they not grow weary or be led astray by any attack or passion. May they find joy in the journey, and may their actions and words present a holy example to those who do not know You. Grant that they may have right faith, hope in the resurrection and the world to come, and that they will be charitable to all in word and deed. In the name of the Father and the Son and the Holy Spirit, now and ever and unto ages of ages. Amen.

> *Create in me a clean heart, O God,*
> *And renew a steadfast spirit within me.*
> *Do not cast me away from Your presence,*
> *And do not take Your Holy Spirit from me.*
> *Restore to me the joy of Your salvation,*
> *And uphold me by Your generous Spirit.*
> *Then I will teach transgressors Your ways,*
> *And sinners shall be converted to You.*
>   *(Ps. 51:10–13)*

TEMPERANCE

> *But also for this very reason, giving all diligence, add*
> *to your faith virtue, to virtue knowledge, to knowl-*
> *edge self-control, to self-control perseverance, to*

> *perseverance godliness, to godliness brotherly kindness,*
> *and to brotherly kindness love. For if these things are*
> *yours and abound, you will be neither barren nor*
> *unfruitful in the knowledge of our Lord Jesus Christ.*
> *(2 Peter 1:5–8)*

Dear Lord, protect my children against the sin of gluttony. When given the opportunity to overindulge, whether in food or pleasures, let them choose to be self-controlled. Help them to be virtuous that they may bear fruit and grow in the wisdom and knowledge of You. Help them to find joy in moderation, discretion, and forbearance, that they may appreciate and enjoy the blessings You bestow on them daily. Help me to live a self-disciplined life so that I may be a worthy example, one that will lead them to You in everything I do. For You are holy, now and ever and unto ages of ages. Amen.

O Holy Trinity, help my children to lead lives of self-control. Help them to remember to be thankful and to enjoy each blessing You give them. Amen.

— 7 —

Prayers Through the Stages of Motherhood

FIRST-TIME MOTHER

EACH AND EVERY MOTHER GOES THROUGH THE experience of being a first-time mother. Some mothers have more preparation and experience than others. We have each faced moments of confusion, fear, uncertainty, and wonder as we behold the little humans the Lord has allowed into our lives. The Theotokos was a very young first-time mother, chosen to feed, nurture, and train the great I AM. Elizabeth was an older woman with years of life experience under her belt, but not the experience of motherhood. It causes us to sacrifice and love and protect with a fierceness and purpose we didn't know we possessed. Be encouraged as you accept this new blessing of motherhood.

Dearest Lord Jesus, grant me Your strength and wisdom as I stand at the beginning of this motherhood journey. Grant me the wisdom to sift through all the advice and information on how to mother, seeking your guidance in how to parent this precious child. Help me to remember, as I nourish my child, to nourish my soul through prayer and the reading of Your holy Word. For in You is all wisdom, and in You I put my trust. Amen.

> *In this beautiful world there is nothing more cherished, no duty more honorable, no responsibility more sacred, and no task more difficult, than that of motherhood. (From the dedication plaque at Agia Anna Monastery in Dumont, Colorado)*

AS A MOTHER TO LITTLE ONES

Parenting from the Narthex ॐ

It was a long but beautiful day, much cooler than it had been for weeks. His Grace Bishop Basil was in attendance at Liturgy, and it was so sweet to watch him bless the children. He's such a big papa bear with children, if that's okay to say about a bishop.

The children played on the playground, drank too much soda, and, most importantly, missed naps. This last bit didn't

matter much while the playground was available. The children played happily enough, but then it was time for church.
No more smiles and giggles. Sweat-and-dirt-streaked faces
bobbled back and forth as unhappy children entered the
sanctuary. The sugar crash was beginning. As the singing
increased, so did the siren-like whine escaping our youngest child's throat. Little eyebrows knit together, and nothing on the planet was entertaining enough to occupy his
exhausted mind.

So off to the narthex we went. Out to sit on an uncom-
fortable chair with an unhappy baby. Yet the words "Lord
have mercy" still reached my ears. "Amen" still escaped
from my lips. I crossed myself on the inside though my
hands weren't available. And this little one absorbed it all
too. God's word says that His word will not return to Him
empty but will accomplish the purpose for which it was sent
(Is. 55). I believe this happens for mamas in the narthex, or
the cry room, or anywhere else where we only hear wisps of
the Liturgy while tending our little ones.

God is there, even in the narthex. He is still ministering
to the mama soul tending the little ones He's given us. He
doesn't forget about us even there. Enjoy those moments,
and as we sit on the outskirts, let us rejoice in those "incon-
venient" times. When we can accept where we are, *there* we
are worshipping our Lord.

O my God and King, help me to be a peace-bearer in my home. Tending to my little ones takes so much time; help me to focus and order my day in a way that is effective in training and loving them and, most importantly, honoring to You. Help me to use kind words and give loving encouragement. Give me the wisdom to direct these precious little ones to love You. During the trying days, remind me that the investment I make in their lives is worth each sacrifice. In the name of the Father and the Son and the Holy Spirit. Amen.

> But Jesus said, "Let the little children come to Me, and do not forbid them; for of such is the kingdom of heaven." (Matt. 19:14)

As a Mother to Older Children

✚ ✚ ✚ ✚ ✚ ✚ ✚ ✚ ✚ ✚ ✚ ✚

St. Nonna, Mother of St. Gregory the Theologian

Commemorated on August 5

St. Nonna, the mother of St. Gregory the Theologian, was the daughter of Christians named Philotatos and Gorgonia, who raised her in Christian piety. St. Nonna was also an aunt of St. Amphilochius, Bishop of Iconium.

St. Nonna married Gregory of Arianzus, who was a rich landowner in the Arianzus and Nazianzus districts. Unfortunately, the marriage caused great misery for the holy soul of St. Nonna because her husband was a pagan. Eventually, through her prayers, her husband had a vision in his sleep, as a result of which he converted to Christianity.

Gregory went to the First Ecumenical Council at Nicea. He was baptized and was ordained presbyter, then Bishop of

Nazianzus (this was before bishops had to be celibate). He devoted himself totally to the Church. At the same time as his consecration as bishop, St. Nonna was made a deaconess. With the same zeal with which she had raised her children, she now occupied herself in performing works of charity.

"She knew," wrote her son, St. Gregory, "one thing to be truly noble: to be pious and to know from where we have come and where we are going; and that there is one innate and trusty wealth: to use one's substance on God and on the poor, especially the impoverished kin. One woman may be distinguished for frugality, and another for piety, while she, difficult as it is to combine both qualities, excelled all others in both of them. In each she attained the height of perfection, and both were combined in her. She did not permit one duty to interfere with the other, but rather each supported the other. What time and place of prayer ever eluded her? She was drawn to this each day before anything else, and she had complete faith that her prayers would be answered. Although greatly moved by the sorrows of strangers, she never yielded to grief to the extent that she allowed any sound of woe to escape her lips before the Eucharist, or a tear to fall from her eye, or for any trace of mourning to remain on a feast day, though she repeatedly endured many sorrows. She subjected every human thing to God."

Her final years brought St. Nonna many sorrows. In 368, her youngest son, Caesarios, died, and the following year, her daughter died. St. Nonna bore these losses submitting to the will of God. She died at prayer in the temple on August 5, 374.

St. Nonna was a model wife and mother, a remarkable woman who devoted her life to God and the Church without neglecting her other responsibilities.[14]

✢ ✢ ✢ ✢ ✢ ✢ ✢ ✢ ✢ ✢ ✢ ✢

I am blessed by St. Nonna and encouraged by the kind words of her sainted son. Clearly the example of his mother had an eternal impact on his life and the life of the Church through him.

Having older children brings many blessings as well as many challenges. On the one hand, they are more self-sufficient. It can be such a joy to watch them grow and learn and apply their growing knowledge to life situations. We rejoice when we see the fruit of our years of invested training. On the other hand, they have days (sometimes weeks, months, or years) of toddler-like behavior because of the wash of hormones they experience as they go through puberty and start testing boundaries again. For them it is an awakening; for us it is like a second labor, with attitudes and negative behaviors hitting us like contractions until we get to the final moment of transition and "birth" them into adulthood. Let our prayers be like cleansing breaths, helping us to manage each "contraction" during this new season of motherhood.

O Christ our God, thank You for allowing me to be mother to my older children. Help them to take responsibility for their actions, thoughts, words, and faith. Show me how to interact with them in a way that allows them to continue to learn and grow. Keep me from being a controller, and forgive me if I have not set the boundaries securely enough. Grant me the strength to entrust them to Your loving care as they stand on the brink of adulthood. Help me to encourage them through the growing process and address difficult situations through prayer, obtaining godly counsel and directing them to seek counsel from their spiritual father. Let me not live a life of hypocrisy, advising them to do what I say, not what I do; instead let my example make them long to serve You with their lives. Amen.

> *Train up a child in the way he should go,*
> *And when he is old he will not depart from it. (Prov. 22:6)*

MOTHER OF AN ONLY CHILD

✠ ✠ ✠ ✠ ✠ ✠ ✠ ✠ ✠ ✠ ✠ ✠

St. Elizabeth, Mother of St. John the Baptist

Commemorated on September 5

The Righteous Elizabeth was the mother of the holy Prophet, Forerunner, and Baptist of the Lord, John. She was descended from the lineage of Aaron and was the sister of St. Anna, the mother of the Most Holy Theotokos. The righteous spouses, "walking in all the commandments of the Lord" (Luke 1:6), suffered barren-ness, which in those days was considered a punishment from God. When Elizabeth gave birth to a son, through the inspiration of the Holy Spirit, she announced that his name was John, although no one in their family had this name. When Elizabeth's husband, Zachariah (who had been rendered mute), was asked what the child's name was, he wrote "John" on a tablet. Immediately, the gift of speech returned to him, and inspired by the Holy Spirit, he began to prophesy about his son as the Forerunner of the Lord.

When King Herod heard from the Magi about the birth of the Messiah, he decided to kill all the infants up to two years of age, hoping the newborn Messiah would be among them. Herod knew about John's unusual birth and wanted to kill him, fearing he was the foretold King of the Jews. But Elizabeth hid herself and her infant in the hills. The murderers searched everywhere for John. When she saw their pursuers, Elizabeth began to implore God for their safety, and the hill opened up and concealed her and her infant from harm. Shortly thereafter, Zachariah was serving in the Temple when soldiers entered and tried in vain to learn from him the whereabouts of his son. Refusing to betray this information, Zachariah was murdered. Elizabeth died forty days after her husband, and St. John dwelt in the wilderness until he appeared to the nation of Israel.

Troparion (Tone 2)

> The memory of Your prophets Zachariah and Elizabeth
> We celebrate today, O Lord.
> By their prayers, we beseech You,
> O Christ God, save our souls!

Kontakion (Tone 4)

> As the full moon brightly reflects the light of the sun,
> you reflected the glory of the Messiah, the Light of wisdom!
> With Zachariah you walked in all of the Lord's command-
>   ments, Elizabeth, beloved by God.
> So as we bless you with fitting songs,
> we praise the Lord, the bountiful Light, who enlightens all.[15]

✠   ✠   ✠   ✠   ✠   ✠   ✠   ✠   ✠   ✠   ✠   ✠

Thank You, Lord, for the blessing of my child. Help me to accept whatever children You bring me, whether one or many. Let me be like Your holy mother, humbly accepting whatever You decide is best for the salvation of my soul and that of my child. Teach me how to train my child in Your holy ways, that when he/she is grown he/she will glorify You with his/her whole heart, soul, mind, and strength. Help me to be encouraged and to remember the many servants of Christ who were only children and who are numbered among the saints. For to You we ascribe glory, in the name of the Father and the Son and the Holy Spirit. Amen.

> *My son, hear the instruction of your father,*
> *And do not forsake the law of your mother;*
> *For they will be a graceful ornament on your head,*
> *And chains about your neck. (Prov. 1:8–9)*

MOTHER TO A LARGE FAMILY

✣ ✣ ✣ ✣ ✣ ✣ ✣ ✣ ✣ ✣ ✣ ✣

St. Emilia, Mother of Ss. Basil and Gregory

Commemorated on January 3 (also on May 30)

The holy and righteous Emilia (also Emily or Emmelia) is the mother of St. Basil the Great and several other saints of the Church. She was the daughter of a martyr. She gave birth to ten children, in whom she instilled the Orthodox faith, teaching them to pray and devote their lives to the service of the Church. As a result of her zealous maternal instruction, five of her children are commemorated as saints on the Church calendar: Ss. Macrina, Basil, Peter of Sebaste, Gregory of Nyssa, and Theosebia, a deaconess. Therefore, St. Emilia is often called "the mother of saints."

When her son Naucratius suddenly died at the age of twenty-seven, Emilia was consoled by her eldest daughter, Macrina. Macrina reminded her that it was not befitting to a Christian to "mourn as those who have no hope" and inspired her to hope courageously in the resurrection granted to us by the Pascha of the Lord.

After her children left home, St. Emilia was persuaded by Macrina to forsake the world. Together they founded a monastery for women. Emilia divided the family property among her children. Retaining only some meager possessions, she and Macrina withdrew to a secluded family property in Pontus, picturesquely located on the banks of the Iris River and not far from Saint Basil's wilderness home. A number of liberated female slaves desired to join the pair, and a convent was formed.

After many years, Emilia reached old age and became ill. Her son Peter came to her side. Together with Macrina, he tended to his mother in her last days. As the oldest and the youngest, Macrina and Peter held a special place in Emilia's heart.

Before committing her soul to the Lord, she prayed, "To You, O Lord, I give the first fruits and the tithe of the fruit of my womb. The first fruit is my first-born daughter, and the tithe is this, my youngest son. Let these be for You a rightly acceptable sacrifice, and let Your holiness descend upon them!" St. Emilia was buried as she had requested, beside her husband in the chapel at their estate in Annesi, where Naucratius had also been laid.[16]

✤　✤　✤　✤　✤　✤　✤　✤　✤　✤　✤　✤

Father, Son, and Holy Spirit, one God. Thank You for the blessing of my large family. Thank You for the life of each child You have allowed into this home. Help me as I attempt to attend to the spiritual, physical, and emotional needs of each child. Show me how to spend time with each child, to encourage them all as they strive to follow You. Direct my time and help me to know how to manage it well, allowing You to set the priorities of my home. Help me to get enough rest so that I may be refreshed and joyfully greet each new day in peace. I ask for Your humility to reign in my heart that I may not become offended by thoughtless things that may be said about my large family. Help me to accept the challenge mothering a large family brings as a means to help me work out my own salvation. Amen.

> *Like arrows in the hand of a warrior,*
> *So are the children of one's youth.*
> *Happy is the man who has his quiver full of them;*
> *They shall not be ashamed,*
> *But shall speak with their enemies in the gate.*
> *(Ps. 127:4–5)*

As a Mother to Adopted & Foster Children

✝ ✝ ✝ ✝ ✝ ✝ ✝ ✝ ✝ ✝ ✝ ✝ ✝

St. Sophia the Mother of Orphans

Celebrated June 2

Mothers of foster and adopted children tend to have some unique life experiences and challenges, from the comments we receive to the very real parenting hurdles we have to jump over because of the ways the lives of our children were influenced or affected before they came into our homes.

St. Sophia the Mother of Orphans was a very loving and devoted Christian wife and mother to six biological children. When she was thirty-four, her area of the world was hit by a plague, and her heart was broken in two when one by one her children, and finally her husband, succumbed to illness. She prayed that God would allow her to follow her beloved family in death, but He had a different plan for her.

In the midst of her sorrow this holy mama was given "beauty for ashes, the oil of joy for mourning, the garment of praise for the spirit of heaviness" (Is. 61:3). She gave away her possessions, keeping only enough to maintain her house, which became a haven for society's outcasts, especially children. Over the course of her life she adopted over one hundred children, raising each as her own and sending them out into the world as lovers of Christ and upstanding citizens.

Holy Saint Sophia, pray for us!

✠   ✠   ✠   ✠   ✠   ✠   ✠   ✠   ✠   ✠   ✠   ✠

James 1:27 reminds us of the importance of looking after (or visiting, depending on the translation) widows and orphans. This action, we are told, is what God considers pure and undefiled religion.

My husband and I have been doing foster care for nine years. There have been many ups and downs along the way. Recently I've had the delightful opportunity to meet some other foster/adoptive parents who get unusual comments from friends and strangers, or get completely ignored (by friends and strangers) as they go through the struggle of raising and caring for some of these children. I think people tend to be unsupportive because they don't understand who these children are or why we would purposefully choose to jump into the uncertain waters of parenting children we did not birth ourselves, so I thought I'd explain my reasons.

The "why" came with our first foster baby, a six-day-old, precious blonde, blue-eyed baby girl. She was not some little deformed monster who screamed all the time (which wouldn't have changed my love for her if she had been); she was a temporary orphan. She had no one, outside of our home, to care for her, hold her, and love her until she could return home or, in her case, into the loving care of relatives.

Our second, third, and fourth foster children have become our sons and have their own stories I will not share now. Number Five was born addicted to heroin and spent the first two weeks out of the hospital going through withdrawal. He didn't scream or cry a lot, he would just shake or twitch. Number Six was on morphine for the first several months of his life because his withdrawal would have been too painful.

Little Mr. Seven was only five weeks old when I picked him up from the children's hospital near us. There, in a huge hospital bed, was a tiny little guy wearing a splint from his hips down because he had two broken femurs and a broken tibia. Number Eight was with us for a short time before being reunited with his brother at his forever home. Number Nine was a delight and would start smacking his lips each time he saw his bottle. Number Ten just needed a place to "hang" while his mama did some hard work. Number Eleven had been thrown off a balcony and came to us, eighteen months old, with twenty-six staples in his head after brain surgery and a month-long stay in the hospital.

Numbers Twelve, Thirteen, Fourteen, and Fifteen were only with us for a few days each because family was found quickly. Number Sixteen was also on morphine for her first few months and had the sweetest little smile. We had the blessing of seeing her get adopted by her wonderful aunt and uncle on the very same day we adopted two of our boys. Number Seventeen was eighteen months old when he came and very detached. It took three months to get him to smile. Number Eighteen stayed only two nights, Nineteen stayed three months, and Twenty stayed a year.

A brother and sister came as Twenty-one and Twenty-two, the littler on oxygen with an inability to self-soothe. Her first smile was such a treat! Sweet Number Twenty-three was just over a year old and slept for almost two days straight as he came down from intentional drug exposure by his parents and some of their friends. Busy Mr. Twenty-four took our family on quite a roller coaster ride with developmental delays and huge bio-family issues. Twenty-five was so tiny until we plumped him up.

Twenty-six is now officially ours, and twenty-seven is in the process of becoming a permanent member of our family. Twenty-eight and Twenty-nine were twins, one of whom had had a heart attack at five months old, and Number Thirty is just a sweet little pink rosebud my nine-year-old has decided to call Rose or Princess Celeste—though neither is her name.

That is why I do what I do. I live for the first smile, laugh, developmental or emotional hurdle reached. Each of these children has been an orphan, whether for hours, days, months, or permanently. And because they have been in our home, each of those children is prayed for the rest of their lives. All but Number Eighteen made it to church to hear about Jesus. We hope their visits will make an impact on someone in the church or the community who will have a little place in their hearts and pray for these little ones who are so close to the heart of Christ.

I do not think everyone should do foster care or adopt children, but *everyone* is charged to care for the widows and orphans. We can fulfill that charge by praying for them, babysitting for a foster or adoptive family, listening with compassion to the trials many of us face by bringing injured (emotionally, physically, or mentally) children into our home. The call is not only to those who take these children physically into their homes; it is for all of us. Let us all be willing to answer that call, for, as God's children, we also have been adopted and made sons and daughters of the King of kings.

Thank You, Holy Father God, for adopting us and making us Your sons and daughters. Help me as I mother these precious children You have allowed into my home. Let me not grow weary as I help them work through the trauma they have experienced. Remind me not to take hurtful words or actions personally. Open my heart during the trying times so I can love them the way You love them. Grant me insight that I might see the heart of the different issues that arise, and give me the wisdom to help them over each hurdle they face. Help my heart to fully embrace my adopted children as You have welcomed us as Your sons and daughters in our brokenness. For You are blessed unto ages of ages. Amen.

Holy Saint Sophia, pray for us. You were mother to hundreds; pray that we will receive these few with joy. Pray the Lord's blessing on each of my foster children, *(Names)*, and ask that healing will take place in their homes or, if that is not possible, that a godly and loving forever home will become available. Pray that I will be open to accepting whomever the Lord brings to my home and that I will freely pour out the love Christ has placed in my heart that they may someday come to know Him. Amen.

> *For as many as are led by the Spirit of God, these are sons of God. For you did not receive the spirit of bondage again to fear, but you received the Spirit of adoption by whom we cry out, "Abba, Father." The Spirit Himself bears witness with our spirit that we are children of God, and if children, then heirs—heirs of God and joint heirs with Christ, if indeed we suffer with Him, that we may also be glorified together. (Rom. 8:14–17)*

PRAYERS FOR YOUR HUSBAND & MARRIAGE

Marriage is one of the Sacraments of the Church. It is more than a decision or a feeling. It is a covenant made before

God and man. Often times, when we struggle in marriage it is because our pride becomes injured or that feeling we call love doesn't seem to be present. But love is more than that. Love endures the bad breath in the morning, the clothes on the floor, and the toothpaste tube being squeezed from the middle. It withstands arguments, sickness, and poverty. By keeping Christ present in the marriage, we can trust Him to be the fortress built around ourselves and our husbands. He is the One we can seek when everything seems to be falling apart, and the One we can praise as we grow together in faith, hope, and love.*

The crowns in an Orthodox marriage ceremony represent the crowns of martyrdom. They remind us that marriage is not simply a remedy for lust or the end of a Christian fairy tale. It is a blessed mystery and a life of willing sacrifice. In marriage there are many trials and challenges. Let us endeavor to cling to Christ and to each other as we serve Him together in this blessed covenantal sacrament.

✣ ✣ ✣ ✣ ✣ ✣ ✣ ✣ ✣ ✣ ✣ ✣

St. Juliana of Lazarevo

Commemorated on January 2

Righteous Juliana of Lazarevo is an astonishing example of a self-denying Christian woman. She was the daughter of a

---

* If you are in a physically or emotionally abusive marriage, do not remain silent. Seek help from your priest or other authority.

nobleman. From her early years she lived devoutly, kept the fasts, and set aside the majority of her time for prayer. Early on, having become orphaned, she was given over into the care of relatives, who laughed at her. Juliana bore everything with patience and without complaint. Her love for people was expressed by nursing the sick and sewing clothing for the poor.

Her pious and virtuous life attracted the attention of Yurii Osoryin, who soon married her. Her husband's parents loved their gentle daughter-in-law and left the running of the household in her hands. Domestic concerns did not disrupt Juliana's spiritual efforts. She always found time for prayer, and she was always prepared to feed the orphaned and clothe the poor. During a harsh famine, she herself remained without food, having given away her last morsel to a beggar. When an epidemic began, Juliana devoted herself completely to the nursing of the sick.

Righteous Juliana had six sons and a daughter. After the death of two of her sons, she wanted to withdraw to a monastery, but her husband persuaded her to remain in the world and continue to raise their children. On the testimony of Juliana's son, Kallistrat Osoryin, who wrote of her life, she became all the more strict with herself. She intensified her fasting and prayer, slept no more than two hours at night, and then would only lay her head on a board.

Upon the death of her husband, Juliana distributed to the poor her portion of the inheritance. Living in extreme poverty, she was nonetheless vivacious and cordial, and in everything she thanked the Lord. When Righteous Juliana fell asleep in the Lord, she was buried beside her husband at the Church of St. Lazarus. In 1614, the relics of Righteous Juliana were uncovered, exuding a fragrant myrrh, from which many received healing.

Troparion (Tone 4)

> By your righteous deeds you revealed to the world
> An image of the perfect servant of the Lord.
> By your fasting, vigil, and prayers,

You were inspired in your evangelical life,
Feeding the hungry and caring for the poor,
Nursing the sick and strengthening the weak.
Now you stand at the right hand of the Master, Christ,
O holy Juliana, interceding for our souls.

✠   ✠   ✠   ✠   ✠   ✠   ✠   ✠   ✠   ✠   ✠   ✠

Traditional Prayer for a Married Couple ☙

O Merciful God, we beseech You ever to remind us that the married state is holy, and that we must keep it so. Grant us Your grace, that we may continue in faithfulness and love. Increase in us the spirit of mutual understanding and trust, that no quarrel or strife may come between us. Grant us Your blessings, that we may stand before our fellows and in Your sight as an ideal family. And finally, by Your mercy, account us worthy of everlasting life: For You are our sanctification, and to You we ascribe glory, to the Father and to the Son and to the Holy Spirit, now and ever and unto ages of ages. Amen.

Prayer by Archimandrite Nicodim (Mandita) ☙

O Lord Jesus Christ our God, our sweet Savior, who taught us to pray always for each other, so that by thus fulfilling the holy law we will be made worthy of Your mercy: look down with compassion on our married life and keep from all perilous falls, from enemies both visible and invisible, my husband/wife whom You have granted me, that we may pass our time together until the end with oneness of mind. Grant him/her health, strength, and fullness of wisdom enlightened from above, so that he/she may be able to fulfill his/her duties all the days of this life according to Your will and commandments.

Protect and keep him/her from temptations, and may he/she be able to bear and conquer those temptations that come upon him/her. Strengthen him/her in right faith, strong hope, and perfect love, so that together we may do good deeds and that we may order all our life according to Your divine ordinances and commandments.

O greatly merciful Lord, hear us who humbly pray to You, and send Your divine blessing in truth on our married life and on all our good deeds, for it is Yours to hear and have mercy on us, O our God, and to You we ascribe glory: to the Father and to the Son and to the Holy Spirit, both now and ever and unto ages of ages. Amen.

O Christ our God, thank You for my husband. Thank You for the talents and skills You have placed in Him. Help me to love him unconditionally and to be an encouragement to him. When challenges come, allow us to face them together with mutual respect. Let my help to him be as an offering to You, O Lord, and let him love me as You love Your Church. Grant us protection from any external or internal attack that would compromise the covenant we made. Help me to be quick to forgive any shortcomings, remembering that we are both in need of Your salvation. Grant us the strength to endure any trial or temptation, drawing closer together and closer to You. For You are our Light and Salvation, and to You we ascribe glory, to the Father and Son and Holy Spirit. Amen.

Wives, submit to your own husbands, as to the Lord.
For the husband is head of the wife, as also Christ is
head of the church; and He is the Savior of the body.

> *Therefore, just as the church is subject to Christ, so*
> *let the wives be to their own husbands in everything.*
> *Husbands, love your wives, just as Christ also loved*
> *the church and gave Himself for her, that He might*
> *sanctify and cleanse her with the washing of water*
> *by the word, that He might present her to Himself*
> *a glorious church, not having spot or wrinkle or any*
> *such thing, but that she should be holy and without*
> *blemish. So husbands ought to love their own wives as*
> *their own bodies; he who loves his wife loves himself.*
> *(Eph. 5:22–28)*

PRAYERS OF A GRANDMOTHER

✢ ✢ ✢ ✢ ✢ ✢ ✢ ✢ ✢ ✢ ✢ ✢

St. Anna, Holy Righteous Ancestor of God

Commemorated on September 9

St. Anna lived with her husband, Joachim, at Nazareth in Galilee. They were childless into their old age and grieved over this. They had to endure derision and scorn, since at that time childlessness was considered a disgrace. They never complained, but fervently prayed to God, humbly trusting in Him.

During a great feast, the gifts Joachim took to the Temple as an offering to God were not accepted by the priest, who considered that a childless man was not worthy to offer sacrifice to God. This pained Joachim, and he decided to settle in solitude in a desolate place. When St. Anna learned what humiliation her husband had endured, she sorrowfully entreated God with prayer and fasting to grant her a child. In his solitude, the righteous Joachim also asked God for a child.

The prayer of the saintly couple was heard. An angel told them that a daughter would be born to them who would be blessed above all other women. The angel also told them that she would remain a virgin, would be dedicated to the Lord and live in the Temple, and would give birth to the Savior. Obeying the instructions of the heavenly messenger, Ss. Joachim and Anna met at the Golden Gate in Jerusalem. Then, as God promised, a daughter was born to them, and they named her Mary.

St. Joachim died a few years later at the age of eighty after Mary went to live in the Temple. St. Anna died at the age of seventy, two years after her husband. Ss. Joachim and Anna are often invoked by couples trying to have children.

Troparion (Tone 4)

> Since you were righteous under the law of grace, O Joachim and Anna,
> For our sake you gave birth to the God-given Infant.
> The divine Church today therefore feasts radiantly,
> Joyfully celebrating your honorable memory and giving glory to God
> Who has raised up a horn of salvation from the house of David!

Kontakion (Tone 3)

> Now Anna is no longer barren and nurses the All-Pure One!
> She rejoices and calls us to sing a hymn of praise to Christ,
> Who gave mankind the only Ever-Virgin Mother!

✠ ✠ ✠ ✠ ✠ ✠ ✠ ✠ ✠ ✠ ✠ ✠

O God of my salvation, grant salvation and protection to my children and grandchildren. Let me be faithful in prayer and an encouragement to my children as they parent their children. Help my grandchildren to honor their parents, to be respectful, and to love the Lord with their whole hearts, minds, and bodies. Keep them from following any false beliefs. Surround them with friends dedicated to Your service. For You are holy, now and ever and unto ages of ages. Amen.

Holy Saint Anna, Grandmother of our Savior, pray for my grandchildren. You held in your womb the one who would become mother to the Church of Christ. Pray for my grandchildren, that they may lead righteous lives and follow Christ wherever He may lead. Pray that His face may shine upon them and they may know Him as Lord. Amen.

> *Children's children are the crown of old men,*
> *And the glory of children is their father. (Prov. 17:6)*

PRAYER OF A SINGLE MOTHER

✛ ✛ ✛ ✛ ✛ ✛ ✛ ✛ ✛ ✛ ✛ ✛

St. Sophia and Her Three Daughters

Commemorated on September 17

The Holy Martyrs Saint Sophia and her daughters Faith, Hope, and Love were from Italy. Sophia was a pious Christian widow who named her daughters for the three great Christian virtues. At the time of their martyrdom, Faith was twelve, Hope was ten, and Love was nine. St. Sophia raised them in the love of the Lord Jesus Christ, and they did not hide their faith, openly confessing it before everyone.

An official named Antiochus denounced them to Emperor Hadrian, who ordered that they be brought to Rome. The holy virgins prayed fervently to the Lord, asking that He give them the strength not to fear torture and death. When they appeared before the emperor, all those present were amazed at their composure. Summoning each of the sisters in turn, Hadrian urged them to offer sacrifice to the goddess Artemis, but the girls remained unyielding.

The emperor then ordered them to be tortured. After undergoing unspeakable torments, the holy virgins glorified their Heavenly Bridegroom and remained steadfast in the Faith.

St. Sophia was subjected to another type of grievous torture: she was forced to watch the suffering of her daughters. She displayed adamant courage and urged her daughters to endure their torments for the sake of the Heavenly Bridegroom. All three maidens were beheaded and joyfully bent their necks beneath the sword.

In order to intensify St. Sophia's suffering, the emperor permitted her to take the bodies of her daughters for burial. She buried them on a high hill beyond the city. After sitting by their graves for three days, she gave up her soul to the Lord. Even though she did not suffer for Christ in the flesh, she was not deprived of a martyr's crown. Instead, she suffered in her heart. Believers buried her body there beside her daughters.

Troparion (Tone 5)
> You blossomed in the courts of the Lord
> as a fruitful olive tree, holy martyr Sophia;
> in your contest you offered to Christ the sweet fruit of your
>   womb,
> your daughters Faith, Hope, and Love.
> Together with them, intercede for us all.

Kontakion (Tone 1)
> The holy branches of noble Sophia,
> Faith, Hope, and Love,
> confounded Greek sophistry through Grace.
> They struggled and won the victory
> and have been granted an incorruptible crown
> by Christ, the Master of all.[17]

✢ ✢ ✢ ✢ ✢ ✢ ✢ ✢ ✢ ✢ ✢ ✢

Prayer of a Single Parent ఌ

Lord Jesus Christ my God, who carried Your own Holy Cross to Golgotha, grant me the strength, patience, and wisdom to bear the burdens of parenthood. Fulfill in me anything I may be lacking, and grant that through our prayers and those of Your Holy Mother, our family may grow closer to You and a life in Christ. Amen.[18]

Dear Holy Father, grant me strength to parent as a single mother. Help me to face each new challenge with the faith that You will lead my steps. I thank You for my children and ask that You grant peace to my heart and home and to the hearts of my children. Grant also, O Lord, freedom from bitterness and despair. If my children are despairing because of life's circumstances, lead them to Your holy temple that they may find peace and healing. In the name of the Father and the Son and the Holy Spirit. Amen.[19]

— 8 —

Prayers for Godchildren & "Bonus" Children

GODCHILDREN

S<small>AINT</small> P<small>RISCILLA</small>, along with her husband Aquila, mentored fellow Christians in the faith so they could gain understanding and tell others about the faith with confidence and accuracy. Being a godparent doesn't mean you have perfected your faith, but that you are actively working out your salvation with fear and trembling. You are coming up alongside the parents and tending to the spiritual growth of your godchild. It is a wonderful and terrifying responsibility. Take heart. Seek God. Pray.

Dear Lord, help me as I embrace my role as godmother. Grant that I will be faithful in prayer and the spiritual education of my godchildren. Bring them to my mind often that they may be constantly covered in prayer. Help me to develop a relationship with them, if possible, and let my life be a godly example for them. Let me tend to my own spiritual growth, that when they have questions about the faith I will be ready to answer and encourage them on the path of their own salvation. In the name of the Father and the Son and the Holy Spirit. Amen.

Responsibilities of the Godparent ᦟ

The responsibilities of the godparent only begin at baptism. The role really expands and hopefully blossoms as the godparent and godchild develop a close and loving relationship. As with any relationship, this spiritual one needs to be fostered and cared for in order for it to develop. The best way for this relationship to grow is through prayer. Pray for your godchild and his or her parents, and the parents should encourage their child to pray for the godparents. By doing this you are encouraging a relationship and giving it the spiritual basis on which to mature.

Here are some practical ideas offered by the Orthodox Church in America website (http://www.oca.org) and Fr. Timothy Sawchak of Ss. Peter & Paul Orthodox Church in Lakewood, Ohio:

1. Celebrate the anniversary of the baptism with a card or a telephone call. Along with learning about the child's patron saint, learn about the saint whose feast day is

celebrated on the date of his or her baptism and share the story of that saint's life with your godchild.

2. Model your faith through your actions. Understand the sacraments as well as the teachings of the Church so that you will be able to answer questions your godchild may have.

3. Encourage the faith life through the types of gifts you give your godchild. Some examples of gifts are a Bible, prayer book, books on the lives of saints, prayer rope, etc. By doing this you are giving tools to help your godchild grow in the faith and are helping him/her to start a personal library of Orthodox teachings.

4. If you live in close proximity to your godchild, make yourself available to spend time with him or her. Find out when school activities and sports events are scheduled and try to go to a few. Plan a special time, whether for lunch or a trip to the zoo, to be with your godchild. These times together will help to make your relationship closer.

5. If you live far away, call, write, or e-mail your godchild. Send a letter at the beginning of a church season (Advent, Lent, etc.) to let him or her know that you will be praying for him. If possible, plan visits to see your godchild.

6. From the moment of Baptism, your godchild deserves a very special place in your prayers, for on the day of judgment you will be asked about your godchild's soul.

7. A faithful godparent will be a friend in Christ and maintain close contact with his godchild. The focus at all times is to progress the child in the knowledge and practice of the Orthodox Faith. The godparent should at all times model a Christlike example. The relationship between the godparent and the baptized is so important and so close that the Church forbids marriage between the godparent and godchild.

8. Pray through the ups and downs of life with your godchild. Find out what's troubling or challenging your godchild, what he or she is excited about or eagerly anticipating, then do your best to talk about God in that context. Encourage your godchild to pray, pray together, and let your godchild know that you are praying for him or her every day.

9. Make a big deal of your godchild's nameday. Celebrate with a special visit and dinner if you're nearby, and give a spiritually oriented gift to celebrate, like an age-appropriate book of his patron saint's life, a new icon, etc.

10. Emphasize the spiritual aspects of holidays. Make it a tradition to read the stories of the Nativity and

Pascha morning with your godchild, and help his or her parents downplay the material and commercial aspects (Santa, the Easter Bunny, loads of loot in pretty wrapping). Play up the feasts of the Church instead— by bringing candles to be blessed at the Feast of the Presentation and flowers at the Dormition of the Theotokos and sharing them with your godchild, or by baking birthday cakes for the nativities of the Theotokos, Jesus, and St. John the Baptist.

11.　Invite your godchild to go with you to Great Vespers, Matins, or weekday services for the feasts if you live close by. Encourage your whole "god-family" to come to church for services other than the Sunday Divine Liturgy, if they don't do so regularly.

12.　Ask what your godchild is learning in church school. Discuss the lesson of the week, and offer to help with church school homework, prepare for oratorical competition or catechism bowl, etc. Buy your godchild's first Bible and update it regularly as his or her reading level increases. Encourage him or her to study the Gospel.

13.　Help your godchild serve God. Choose a service project to work at regularly together, such as working at a hot-meal program or visiting parishioners in the hospital. Help him or her discover new ways to use

God-given talents to help others—the artistic might design posters or programs for retreats, the musical might record church music for shut-ins, etc. Encourage your godsons to serve in the altar, too.

14. Encourage both boys and girls to attend seminary and explore the monastic lifestyle, if they show interest. Mention the priesthood as a career choice to your godsons, and help them learn more about what our Orthodox clergy do—and how important their calling to guide others in the Faith is to all of us.

15. Make your godchild one of the family. Include your godchild, and his or her parents and siblings, in your own family's social events: reunions, picnics, camping trips, and zoo and museum outings.

16. Spend time together. Keep in touch by phone, e-mail, or postcard if your godchildren are out of state or across the globe. Prayer and love in Christ know no distance!

> *Therefore, brethren, having boldness to enter the*
> *Holiest by the blood of Jesus, by a new and living way*
> *which He consecrated for us, through the veil, that*
> *is, His flesh, and having a High Priest over the house*
> *of God, let us draw near with a true heart in full*
> *assurance of faith, having our hearts sprinkled from an*
> *evil conscience and our bodies washed with pure water.*
> *Let us hold fast the confession of our hope without*

> *wavering, for He who promised is faithful. And let*
> *us consider one another in order to stir up love and*
> *good works, not forsaking the assembling of ourselves*
> *together, as is the manner of some, but exhorting one*
> *another, and so much the more as you see the Day*
> *approaching. (Heb. 10:19–25)*

STEPCHILDREN

Did you ever think of the fact that the Theotokos was a stepmother? I hadn't either until a dear friend pointed it out to me. Joseph was a widower who already had children. We don't know to what extent she may have mothered Joseph's children, but the Bible attests to the fact that she did have interactions with them—thirty-three years' worth of interaction, before the death of Jesus. It is a big responsibility to step into a marriage where you pick up the role of stepmother. You may be seen as a blessing or a challenge or the enemy. Whatever level of interaction you have with these precious children, you have the wonderful privilege of praying for them as they work through their own challenges in life.

Dear Lord, show me how to interact with my "bonus" children in such a way that they feel loved but not threatened. Help me to trust You for direction and protect my heart from any direct or indirect insults and challenges that may come my way. Instead, let me be diligent in prayer for these precious children, because though they are not mine, You have placed them in my life to love and pray for all the days of their lives. Let me be an encourager to them and a person they can learn to trust. In the name of the Father and the Son and the Holy Spirit. Amen.

> *Love suffers long and is kind; love does not envy; love does not parade itself, is not puffed up; does not behave rudely, does not seek its own, is not provoked, thinks no evil; does not rejoice in iniquity, but rejoices in the truth; bears all things, believes all things, hopes all things, endures all things. (1 Cor. 13:4–7)*

Prayers for the Future

"Therefore do not worry, saying, 'What shall we eat?' or 'What shall we drink?' or 'What shall we wear?' For after all these things the Gentiles seek. For your heavenly Father knows that you need all these things. But seek first the kingdom of God and His righteousness, and all these things shall be added to you. Therefore do not worry about tomorrow, for tomorrow will worry about its own things. Sufficient for the day is its own trouble." (Matt. 6:31–34)

RELATIONSHIP WITH CHRIST AND THE CHURCH

Brothers and Sisters! The all-merciful God desires happiness for us, both in this life and in the life to come. To this end He established His Holy Church, so that she might cleanse us from sin, sanctify us, reconcile us with Him and give us a heavenly blessing. The

embrace of the Church is always open to us. Let
us all hasten there more quickly, we whose consciences
are burdened. Let us hasten, and the Church will lift
the weight of our burdens, give us boldness before God,
and fill our hearts with happiness and blessedness.
(St. Nectarius of Aegina)

O Lord Jesus Christ, I bring my child/ren *(Names)* before You and ask Your protection and mercy concerning their relationship with You and Your Church. Help them to be attentive in services, participating with true love for You. Let them be sensitive to the leading of the Holy Spirit, and let their hearts long for a living relationship with You and Your Church. May they seek refuge in Your Word and participate regularly in the sacraments of the Church. May they serve with joy and willingly attend to the needs within the Church. Draw them unto Yourself that they may follow You all the days of their lives. In the name of the Father and the Son and the Holy Spirit, now and ever and unto ages of ages. Amen.

The Church is holy, although there are sinners within
her. Those who sin, but who cleanse themselves with
true repentance, do not keep the Church from being
holy. But unrepentant sinners are cut off, whether visi-
bly by Church authority, or invisibly by the judgment of
God, from the body of the Church. And so in this regard
the Church remains holy. (Saint Philaret of Moscow)

EDUCATION

Of all holy works, the education of children is the most
holy. (St. Theophan the Recluse)

Dear Lord, bless the education of my children. Help me to instruct them well when they are with me and protect their hearts and minds from any false teaching they may receive while outside of my care. Grant them wisdom, ease of learning, and good homework practices. Help them to be respectful toward their instructors and to always maintain an Orthodox worldview, that they may filter all information they receive through the truth of the Orthodox faith. Help me to be a faithful teacher, using the time I have been given to train them that Your Word may dwell in their hearts. Amen.

> *The primary goal in the education of children is to teach, and to give the example of, a virtuous life. (St. John Chrysostom)*

CAREER

> *Do not think about or do anything without a spiritual purpose, whereby it is done for God. For if you travel without purpose, you shall labor in vain. (St. Mark the Ascetic)*

Our Father in heaven, bless my children as they begin their careers. Let the work they choose glorify You. If they are under the authority of an employer, let them be hard workers and let them be known for their integrity. If they are in a place of authority, let them act with fairness and kindness to those under their leadership. Grant them prosperity, and let them remember to honor You with the giving of tithes and alms. For You are holy, now and ever and unto ages of ages. Amen.

*No matter who you are, what kind of work you
do, give an account of yourself as to how you have
performed your work: as a Christian, or as a heathen
(that is, motivated by self-love and worldly pleasure).
A Christian must remember that every deed, even
the smallest, has a moral principle. A Christian,
who remembers the teaching of Jesus Christ, should
perform every deed so that it will be of use toward
the spreading of the grace of God and the Kingdom of
Heaven among men. (St. Gabriel of Imereti)*

PRAYER FOR YOUR CHILD
IN MARRIAGE

*Husbands, never call her simply by her name, but
with terms of endearment, with honor, with much
love. Honor her, and she will not need honor from
others; she will not want the glory that comes from
others, if she enjoys that which comes from you.
Prefer her before all, on every account, both for her
beauty and her discernment, and praise her. (St. John
Chrysostom)*

Dear Lord Jesus, You created man and woman and the sacrament of marriage. Bless my children with spouses who truly serve You as King of their hearts and lives. Grant that together they may faithfully participate in the sacraments and the life of the Church. Let them faithfully honor one another and keep the marriage bed holy. Let them speak to each other with kindness, encouraging one another in the faith. And remind them to faithfully pray for one another that the enemy may gain no foothold. For You are a good God and love mankind. Amen.

A house is a little church . . . let your prayers be com-
mon. Let each go to Church; and let the husband ask
his wife at home, and she again ask her husband, the
account of the things which were said and read there.
. . . Teach her that there is nothing in life that is to be
feared, save only offending against God. If any marry
thus, with these views, he will be but little inferior to
monks. (St. John Chrysostom)

PRAYERS FOR YOUR CHILD
AS A FATHER OR MOTHER

The best inheritance you can leave your sons, the
richest dowry you can prepare for your daughters, is a
truly Christian upbringing. (Bishop Irenaeus)

O gracious Lord Jesus, help my children to be godly parents.
Help them to be faithful in the instruction of the faith, placing the salvation of their children at the very forefront of their
parenting. Let them be gentle and free from anger, full of love,
with an abundance of mercy. Let them be consistent and fair
in discipline, constantly seeking Your insight. Remind them to
pray for their children and to be diligent in their commitment
to the faith. In the name of the Father and the Son and the
Holy Spirit. Amen.

Let us raise our children in such a way that they can
face any trouble, and not be surprised when diffi-
culties come; let us bring them up in the discipline
and instruction of the Lord. . . . When we teach our
children to be good, to be gentle, to be forgiving, to
be generous, to love their fellow men, to regard this

present age as nothing, we instill virtue in their souls,
and reveal the image of God within them. This, then,
is our first task: to educate both ourselves and our chil-
dren in godliness; otherwise what answer will we have
before Christ's judgment seat? (St. John Chrysostom)

IF YOUR CHILD IS CALLED
TO PRIESTHOOD OR MONASTICISM

A lovely abbess I speak with said:

> *It is a rare parent who can rejoice in offering their child*
> *to the Lord. It is most often viewed as a great sorrow*
> *or even a disaster. The hope of being grandparents, or*
> *being near one's adult married child is a natural and even*
> *blessed hope (as mentioned in the Mystery of Marriage*
> *Service), but it is rare that a parent truly understands*
> *that the child already belongs to the Lord, and that the*
> *Lord made the child so in his mother's womb. If parents*
> *(as you know better than I) raise their children up unto*
> *the Lord, and to serve the Church then the sacrifice*
> *becomes much easier, and the parents are able to bless the*
> *child for their monastic life.*

It is difficult to have to rethink the future, but we are
to trust the One who held it in His hands in the first place.
Let us, then, rejoice that our children desire the Kingdom of
God to the extent that they are willing to leave this world
behind and wait at the very door to the Kingdom until the
Bridegroom bids them enter. To God be the glory!

Our Father who art in heaven,
Hallowed be Your name.
Your kingdom come.
Your will be done
On earth as it is in heaven.
Give us this day our daily bread.
And forgive us our trespasses,
As we forgive those who trespass against us.
And lead us not into temptation,
But deliver us from the evil one. (Matt. 6:9–13)

Prayer for a Son Entering the Priesthood ꙩ

Blessed Lord Jesus, grant clarity of heart and mind to my son who desires to become a priest. Place people into his life who can offer godly guidance. Give my son the wisdom to know whether he should pursue the priesthood in celibacy. If Your desire is for him to marry, provide a woman who also embraces the call You have put on his life. Grant him the wisdom to protect his heart and mind from any unbeneficial influence and to avoid every temptation, strengthening him so that he will be prepared when temptations come, as they do to those striving to shepherd Your sheep. Let him live, learn, and preach Your word in all humility. If he partakes of the sacrament of marriage, protect his family and let him not neglect the upbringing of his own children. Amen.

Prayer for a Child Entering Monasticism ꙩ

O Omnipotent Father, bless my child who feels called into Your service. Thank You for the desire You have placed in my child's heart to work out his/her salvation in this way. Grant clear direction and godly counsel concerning this call. Help me to offer my child into Your service with joy and gladness, like Hannah, who gave her firstborn, Samuel, to the temple, or Saint Anna, who willingly surrendered her long-prayed-for daughter to Your loving care so she could become the mother of all. Help me to be willing to relinquish the hope of having grandchildren and to assist my child in following Your voice. Grant my child the strength to follow where You lead and the courage to be faithful all of his/her days. Amen.

> Therefore, holy brethren, partakers of the heavenly calling, consider the Apostle and High Priest of our confession, Christ Jesus, who was faithful to Him who appointed Him, as Moses also was faithful in all His house. For this One has been counted worthy of more glory than Moses, inasmuch as He who built the house has more honor than the house. For every house is built by someone, but He who built all things is God. And Moses indeed was faithful in all His house as a servant, for a testimony of those things which would be spoken afterward, but Christ as a Son over His own house, whose house we are if we hold fast the confidence and the rejoicing of the hope firm to the end. (Heb. 3:1–6)

BE ENCOURAGED, NEW MOTHER, AND DO NOT LOSE heart, seasoned mother, or think that the trials you are facing in your calling will disqualify you from the prize. Pray with faith, grandmother; approach the throne room of Christ, dear godmother, for the children you have been entrusted with. The Lord Himself holds your hand and wants you to succeed through His love, by the power of His Cross, through the prayers of His holy Mother and all the saints.

ANNALISA BOYD

ENDNOTES

1   http: anaphorapress.com music education articles-and-essays on-motherhood

2   Published by Saint Ketarios Greek Orthodox Monastery

3   www.orthodoxnet.com

4   http: www.denver.goarch.org clergy resources liturgical metropolis evchologion Ministry_to_the_Sick.pdf (p. 24)

5   These two prayers are taken from http: www.orthodoxprayer.org OtherPrayers.html

6   From *The Book of Needs* (South Canaan, PA: St. Tikhon's Seminary Press), p. 26

7   http: www.orthodoxprayer.org OtherPrayers.html

8   http: www.orthodoxprayer.org OtherPrayers.html

9   http: www.orthodoxprayer.org OtherPrayers.html

10   http: www.memorieshonored.com ?page=orthodoxprayers

11   http: www.orthodoxnet.com worship occasionalprayers.html

12   http: www.orthodoxprayer.org OtherPrayers.html

13   http: www.goarch.org ourfaith ourfaith8476

14   Adapted from www.oca.org

15   Adapted from www.oca.org

16   Adapted from www.orthodoxwiki.org

17   Adapted from www.oca.org

18   http://www.orthodoxprayer.org/Family_Prayers.html

19   *Wounded by Love: The Life and Wisdom of Elder Porphyrios,* trans. by John Raffan (Limni, Evia, Greece: Denise Harvey, Publisher, 2005), p. 196.

ALSO BY ANNALISA BOYD

Hear Me
A Prayerbook for Orthodox Teens

Give your teens the gift that will challenge their faith and help them on the road to making that faith their own. *Hear Me* is a prayer book designed to address the unique challenges Orthodox youth experience in their walk with Christ. This user-friendly manual communicates the importance of both corporate and personal prayer. Prayers for school, friendships, and family give teens tools for successful relationships. A topical section offers encouragement as teens face daily challenges. The Q & A section answers practical questions. *Hear Me* gives teens direction in using the tools Christ has given us—Holy Scripture as the map, and the Church and her Traditions the compass, helping our youth find their own path toward theosis.
• Paperback, 96 pages, ISBN: 978-1-888212-93-8—$8.95*

Special Agents of Christ
A Prayer Book for Young Orthodox Saints

You're never too young to be one of God's "special agents"—the people He uses to accomplish His will in the world. In this prayer book written especially for middle-grade children, the author of the popular teen prayer book *Hear Me* uses the examples of special agents of the past—the saints—to encourage children to serve God here and now. In addition to morning and evening prayers, prayers for special needs, and psalms to pray, *Special Agents of Christ* includes "training drills" on preparing for confession, understanding the Liturgy and the clergy's vestments, and more.
• Paperback, 96 pages, ISBN: 978-1-936270-55-2—$10.95*

*Available from store.ancientfaith.com

Recommended Reading

The Scent of Holiness
Lessons from a Women's Monastery
by Constantina Palmer

Every monastery exudes the scent of holiness, but women's monasteries have their own special flavor. Join Constantina Palmer as she makes frequent pilgrimages to a women's monastery in Greece and absorbs the nuns' particular approach to their spiritual life. If you're a woman who's read of Mount Athos and longed to partake of its grace-filled atmosphere, this book is for you. Men will find it a fascinating read as well.

• Paperback, 88 pages, ISBN 978-1-936270-42-2 — $18.95*

Close to Home
One Orthodox mother's quest for patience, peace, and perseverance
by Molly Sabourin

Close to Home is for every young mother who's ever wished children came with an instruction manual; who's ever longed for just one quiet minute to finish a thought or utter a prayer; who's ever despaired of perfecting herself in time to become a good example for her children. With courage, humor, and unflinching honesty, Molly addresses all these frustrations and more—offering not answers or solutions, but a new perspective, a pat on the shoulder, a reassuring "I've been there too, and there is hope."

• Paperback, 192 pages, ISBN 978-1-888212-61-7 — $15.95*

Following a Sacred Path
Raising Godly Children
by Elizabeth White

Practical advice for parents (and educators) on raising children to understand and love their faith. Includes activities the family can share that encourage children to discover spiritual truths for themselves and own them for life.

• Paperback, 144 pages, ISBN 978-1-936270-73-6 — $13.95*

In God's Hands
A Mother's Journey through Her Infant's Critical Illness
by Elissa Bjeletich

Popular AFR podcaster Elissa Bjeletich ("Raising Saints") tells the story of her youngest daughter's battle with liver disease, showing how her doubt, fear, and impatience gave way to faith in God's providence.

• Paperback, 256 pages, ISBN 978-1-936270-65-1— $18.95*

Celebrating the Twelve Days of Christmas
A Family Devotional in the Eastern Orthodox Tradition
by AmandaEve Wigglesworth, with illustrations by Grace Brooks

With hymns, stories, meditations, and activities for each day as well as suggestions for the whole season, *Celebrating the Twelve Days of Christmas* provides an invaluable resource for families looking to restore the season of Christmas to its rightful place in their lives.

• Paperback, 48 pages, ISBN 978-1-936270-54-5—$12.95*

A Book of Hours
Meditations on the Traditional Christian Hours of Prayer
by Patricia Colling Egan

Eastern and Western Christians share a rich spiritual heritage in the Hours of Prayer—the brief services of praise and psalmody that mark the progress of each day, sanctifying the hours of our lives. In this gem of a book, Patricia Egan digs deeply into the meaning of each of the Hours, drawing on poetry, nature, experience, and theology to show how the services reflect the different aspects of our salvation and our lives. *A Book of Hours* is an excellent companion for anyone who wants to experience the blessing of praying through the Hours of each day. Inside pages are printed in two colors and feature calligraphy elements by Carla Harris.

• Paperback, 192 pages, ISBN 978-1-936270-06-4—$21.95*

*Prices do not include applicable sales tax or shipping and handling.
Prices were current on April 1, 2014, and are subject to change. To request a catalog, to obtain complete ordering information, or to place a credit card order, please call us at (800) 967-7377 or (219) 728-2216 or log onto our website: store.ancientfaith.com.

Ancient Faith Publishing hopes you have enjoyed and benefited from this book. The proceeds from the sales of our books only partially cover the costs of operating our nonprofit ministry—which includes both the work of **Ancient Faith Publishing** (formerly known as Conciliar Press) and the work of **Ancient Faith Radio**. Your financial support makes it possible to continue this ministry both in print and online. Donations are tax-deductible and can be made at www.ancientfaith.com.

ANCIENT FAITH RADIO

Bringing you Orthodox Christian music, readings, prayers, teaching and podcasts 24 hours a day since 2004 at
www.ancientfaith.com